Cognition and Communication: Judgmental Biases, Research Methods, and the Logic of Conversation

Cognition and Communication: Judgmental Biases, Research Methods, and the Logic of Conversation

Norbert Schwarz
University of Michigan

LEA LAWRENCE ERLBAUM ASSOCIATES, PUBLISHERS
1996   Mahwah, New Jersey

Lawrence Erlbaum Associates, Inc., Publishers
10 Industrial Avenue
Mahwah, New Jersey 07430-2262

Cover design by Mairav Salomon-Dekel

Library of Congress Cataloging-in-Publication Data

Schwarz, Norbert, Dr. phil.
    Cognition and communication : judgmental biases, research
methods, and the logic of conversation
        p.   cm. — (John M. MacEachran memorial lecture series ;
    1995)
    Includes bibliographical references and index.
    ISBN 0-8058-2314-X (cloth : alk. paper)
    1. Judgment. 2. Cognition. 3. Interpersonal communication.
4. Conversation. 5. Human information processing. I. Title. II.
Series.
    BF447.S38 .996
    153.6—dc20   96-31266
                                                      CIP

Books published by Lawrence Erlbaum Associates are printed on
acid-free paper, and their bindings are chosen for strength and
durability

Printed in the United States of America
10 9 8 7 6 5 4 3 2 1

Contents

John M. MacEachran
Memorial Lecture Series

The Department of Psychology at the University of Alberta inaugurated the MacEachran Memorial Lecture Series in 1975 in honor of the late John M. MacEachran. Professor MacEachran was born in Ontario in 1877 and received a PhD in Philosophy from Queen's University in 1905. In 1906 he left for Germany to begin more formal study in psychology, first spending just less than a year in Berlin with Stumpf, and then moving to Leipzig, where he completed a second PhD in 1908 with Wundt as his supervisor. During this period he also spent time in Paris studying under Durkheim and Henri Bergson. With these impressive qualifications the University of Alberta was particularly fortunate in attracting him to its faculty in 1909.

Professor MacEachran's impact has been significant at the university, provincial, and national levels. At the University of Alberta he offered the first courses in psychology and subsequently served as Head of the Department of Philosophy and Psychology and Provost of the University until his retirement in 1945. It was largely owing to his activities and example that several areas of academic study were established on a firm and enduring basis. In addition to playing a major role in establishing the Faculties of Medicine, Education, and Law in the Province, Professor MacEachran was also instrumental in the formative stages of the Mental Health Movement in Alberta. At a national level, he was one of the founders of the Canadian Psychological Association and also became its first Honorary President in 1939. John M. MacEachran was indeed one of the pioneers in the development of psychology in Canada.

Perhaps the most significant aspect of the MacEachran Memorial Lecture Series has been the continuing agreement that the
Department of Psychology at the University of Alberta has with
Lawrence Erlbaum Associates, Publishers, Inc., for the publication
of each lecture series. The following is a list of the Invited Speakers
and the titles of their published lectures:

1975   Frank A. Geldard (Princeton University)
        *Sensory Saltation: Metastability in the Perceptual
        World*

1976   Benton J. Underwood (Northwestern University)
        Temporal Codes for Memories: Issues and Problems

1977   David Elkind (Rochester University)
        The Child's Reality: Three Developmental Themes

1978   Harold Kelley (University of California, Los Angeles)
        Personal Relationships: Their Structures and Processes

1979   Robert Rescorla (Yale University)
        *Pavlovian Second-Order Conditioning: Studies
        in Associative Learning*

1980   Mortimer Mishkin (NIMH-Bethesda)
        Cognitive Circuits (unpublished)

1981   James Greeno (University of Pittsburgh)
        *Current Cognitive Theory in Problem Solving
        (unpublished)*

1982   William Uttal (University of Michigan)
        Visual Form Detection in 3-Dimensional Space

1983   Jean Mandler (University of California, San Diego)
        Stories, Scripts, and Scenes: Aspects of Schema Theory

1984   George Collier and Carolyn Rovee-Collier (Rutgers
        University)
        Learning and Motivation: Function and Mechanism
        (unpublished)

1985   Alice Eagly (Purdue University)
        Sex Differences in Social Behavior: A Social-Role
        Interpretation

1986   Karl Pribram (Stanford University)
        Brain and Perception: Holonomy and Structure
        in Figural Processing

1987   Abram Amsel (University of Texas at Austin)
        Behaviorism, Neobehaviorism, and Cognitivism
        in Learning Theory: Historical and Contemporary
        Perspectives

1988   Robert S. Siegler and Eric Jenkins (Carnegie Mellon
        University)
        How Children Discover New Strategies

1989   Robert Efron (University of California, Martinez)
        The Decline and Fall of Hemispheric Specialization

1990   Philip N. Johnson-Laird (Princeton University)
        Human and Machine Thinking

1991   Timothy A. Salthouse (Georgia Institute of Technology)
        Mechanisms of Age-Cognition Relations in Adulthood

1992   Scott Paris (University of Michigan)
        Authentic Assessment of Children's Literacy
        and Learning

1993   Bryan Kolb (University of Lethbridge)
        Brain Plasticity and Behavior

1995   Norbert Schwarz (University of Michigan)
        Cognition and Communication: Judgmental Biases,
        Research Methods, and the Logic of Conversation

Eugene C. Lechelt, Coordinator
MacEachran Memorial Lecture Series

Sponsored by The Department of Psychology, The University of
Alberta with the support of The Alberta Heritage Foundation for
Medical Research in memory of John M. MacEachran, pioneer in
Canadian psychology.

Acknowledgments

This book is based on a series of talks delivered as the 1995 John M. MacEachran Memorial Lectures at the University of Alberta. I would like to thank the coordinator of the lecture series, Eugene Lechelt, for the invitation and his colleagues at the University of Alberta for an intellectually engaging and stimulating visit. I will long remember the generous hospitality extended by Robert Sinclair, Norman Brown, Michael Enzle, Curt Hoffman, and Sheree Kwong See, who made a cold Albertan autumn a warm experience. The research reported here has greatly benefited from discussions with numerous friends and colleagues. I am particularly indebted to Fritz Strack for many years of collaborative research; much of what is reported here grew out of our joint efforts. I am also grateful to Herbert Bless, Gerd Bohner, Hans-Jürgen Hippler, Bärbel Knäuper, and Michaela Wänke for many fruitful collaborations on related issues. My thinking about conversational processes has been thoroughly influenced by discussions with Tory Higgins and Denis Hilton, who acquainted me with Grice's work. More recently, Daniel Kahneman and Richard Nisbett have provided extremely helpful and stimulating critiques. Many of these colleagues have commented on previous versions of this manuscript and their suggestions were greatly appreciated, although not always heeded. Any inaccuracies that remain are solely my responsibility.

In preparing the present manuscript, I have drawn freely on a chapter published in the Advances in Experimental Social Psychology (Schwarz, 1994) and I thank Academic Press for the permission to use this material in the present book.

—*Norbert Schwarz*

1

Cognition, Communication, and the Fallacies of Human Judgment

To many observers of psychological research, the focus of the field bears an unfortunate resemblance to the scenes depicted in Fig. 1.1: What psychologists seem particularly interested in are the mental processes of individuals studied in social isolation. And whatever these individuals are thinking about, they seem likely to get it wrong as the vast literature on judgmental biases and shortcomings suggests. In this book, I argue that these two observations are not unrelated: Our focus on individual thought processes has fostered a neglect of the social context in which individuals do their thinking and this neglect has contributed to the less than flattering portrait that psychology has painted of human judgment.

To illustrate the scope of the issue, it is helpful to begin with a review of a diverse set of judgmental fallacies. Although the examples may initially strike the reader as unrelated, it will soon become apparent that they share a common theme.

FALLACIES OF HUMAN JUDGMENT

No matter if we form impressions of other people, recall episodes from memory, report our attitudes in an opinion poll, or make important decisions, psychological research suggests that the result is error prone. The errors we make are not trivial and often seem to violate common sense and basic logic. Moreover, minor variations in the research procedures used, or the questions asked, can result in major differences in the obtained results, sometimes suggesting opposite conclusions about the issue under investigation. A few

2

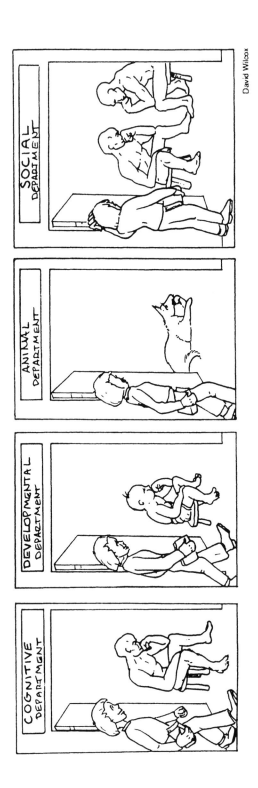

David Wilcox

FIG. 1.1.   Cognitive social psychology (reproduced from *The Psychologist*, July 1988, p. 296 with permission).

examples from different research domains may illustrate some of the more surprising, but reliably replicable, findings.

- We attribute observed behavior to the actor's disposition, even when we are aware of obvious situational pressures that are sufficient to explain the behavior (e.g., Jones & Harris, 1967). This bias is so pervasive it has been called the *fundamental attribution error* (Ross, 1977).
- We rely on nondiagnostic individuating information at the expense of more diagnostic baserate information, concluding, for example, that someone who "likes home carpentry and mathematical puzzles" is most likely an engineer—and our likelihood estimate is hardly influenced by our knowledge about the proportion of engineers in the sample from which the person was drawn (e.g., Kahneman & Tversky, 1973).
- We "recall" things we haven't seen, simply because they were mentioned in a question (e.g., Loftus, 1975).
- Children do not understand that changing the spatial arrangement of objects does not change their number. Although they correctly report that two rows of seven objects each are equal in number when aligned one to one, changing the spatial arrangement of the objects in one row is likely to lead them astray, reflecting a lack of number conservation (e.g., Piaget, 1952).
- When asked a question in an opinion poll, we are happy to report opinions on issues that don't exist. On average, about 30% of any sample reports opinions on issues invented by the researcher (e.g., Schuman & Presser, 1981).
- Our attitude reports are strongly influenced by the numeric values presented on a rating scale. For example, when asked how successful they have been in life, more people report high success when the verbal label "not at all successful" is presented with the numeric value -5 rather than the numeric value 0 (Schwarz, Knäuper, Hippler, Noelle-Neumann, & Clark, 1991).
- Our autobiographical recall of daily behaviors depends on the frequency scale provided. For example, we report watching more television when the frequency scale presented by the researcher provides high rather than low frequency response alternatives (e.g., Schwarz, Hippler, Deutsch, & Strack, 1985).

- Whether our doctor thinks that having headaches twice a week is a serious problem depends on the frequency scale on which the symptom is reported (e.g., Schwarz, Bless, Bohner, Harlacher, & Kellenbenz, 1991).
- Whether the quality of our marriage bears on our general life satisfaction depends on the order in which the two questions are asked, with the correlation between both running anywhere from $r = .1$ to $r = .7$, depending on features of the questionnaire (e.g., Schwarz, Strack, & Mai, 1991).

Depending on researchers' academic discipline and the goal of the investigation, these phenomena are discussed under different headings—including *judgmental biases, shortcomings, measurement errors,* or *artifacts*—and are traced to different underlying processes. Closer inspection reveals, however, that many demonstrations of these and other fallacies share a common feature: Rather than reflecting inherent shortcomings of human judgment, they reflect, in part, that the research procedures on which the findings are based violate the tacit assumptions that govern the conduct of conversation in daily life.

THINKING IN A SOCIAL CONTEXT: THE LOGIC OF CONVERSATION

According to the tacit assumptions that underlie the conduct of conversation, "communicated information comes with a guarantee of relevance" (Sperber & Wilson, 1986, p. vi) and listeners are entitled to assume that the speaker tries to be informative, truthful, relevant, and clear. Moreover, listeners interpret the speakers' utterances "on the assumption that they are trying to live up to these ideals" (Clark & Clark, 1977, p. 122). Bringing these assumptions to the research situation, subjects in psychological experiments and respondents in opinion surveys assume that every contribution of the researcher is relevant to the aims of the ongoing conversation; that every contribution is informative, truthful, and clear; and they refer to the context of the conversation to resolve any ambiguities that may arise. Unfortunately, they miss one crucial point: Whereas the researcher is likely to comply with conversational maxims in almost any conversation he or she conducts outside of a research setting, the researcher is much less likely to do so in the research setting itself. In fact, the researcher may violate each and every maxim of conversation by providing information that is neither relevant, nor truthful, informative, and clear—and may have carefully designed the situation to suggest otherwise. Research participants, however, have no reason to suspect that the researcher is not a cooperative communicator and are hence likely to find meaning in the researcher's contributions.

The findings reviewed in the following chapters suggest that this basic misunderstanding about the cooperative nature of communication in research settings has contributed to some of the more puzzling findings in social and psychological research and is, in part, responsible for the less than flattering picture of human judgmental abilities that has emerged from psychological research. At the outset, however, I emphasize that many of the more robust biases are overdetermined and reflect more than one process. Hence, "getting the communication right" will not necessarily eliminate the phenomena under all conditions. But if we are to understand human judgment in natural contexts, we need to ensure that our experiments do not produce the phenomena for reasons that are unlikely to hold in daily life, where communicators are, indeed, likely to be cooperative participants and where our world knowledge may alert us to situations in which others may be less than fully cooperative. In addition to bearing on methodological issues of social and psychological research, a conversational analysis of judgmental shortcomings has important theoretical implications for the conceptualization of human cognition and judgment by highlighting its inherently social and contextualized nature.

A PREVIEW

Chapter 2 provides an introduction to Grice's (1975) logic of conversation and its extensions by Sperber and Wilson (1986), Clark (e.g., Clark & Schober, 1992) and Higgins and colleagues (e.g., McCann & Higgins, 1992). As previously noted, one of the key tenets of the logic of conversation holds that communicated information comes with a guarantee of relevance. Hence, research participants are likely to search for relevance in the researcher's contributions, rendering logically irrelevant information conversationally relevant. Chapters 3 and 4 review research that illustrates how judgmental biases are attenuated or eliminated once the relevance principle is called into question, thus setting research participants free to ignore some of the information provided to them. Chapter 5 applies a conversational framework to issues of questionnaire construction and reviews what respondents infer from formal features of questionnaires, such as the numbers on a rating scale or other response alternatives provided to them. Rather than reflecting shallow responding or artifacts of psychological measurement, the impact of these features on the obtained responses indicates that research participants draw on all contributions made by the researcher to determine the meaning of the question asked—and these contributions include apparently formal features of questionnaire design.

A second tenet of the logic of conversation holds that speakers are to be informative and are to provide information that is new to the recipient, rather than to reiterate information that the recipient already has, or may take for granted anyway. Chapter 6 traces a wide range of judgmental phenomena to the operation of this nonredundancy principle, including the emergence of question order effects in attitude research and children's apparent inability to master number conservation. Finally, Chapter 7 discusses the methodological and theoretical implications of the reviewed research.

2

Cognition and Communication: The Logic of Conversation

Central to a conversational analysis of human judgment is the distinction between the semantic meaning of a sentence and the pragmatic meaning of an utterance. As Clark and Schober (1992) noted in a related context, it is a "common misperception that language use has primarily to do with words and what they mean. It doesn't. It has primarily to do with people and what they mean. It is essentially about speakers' intentions" (p.15). As the examples in this book illustrates, many of the more surprising shortcomings of human judgment reflect that research participants go beyond the literal meaning of the information provided by the researcher and draw on the pragmatic rather than the semantic meaning of the researcher's contributions. The researcher, however, evaluates participants' judgments against a normative model that draws only on the logical implications of semantic meaning at the expense of the pragmatic implications of the researcher's utterances.

To understand the underlying processes, we need to understand how people determine a speaker's intentions. In general, determining the intended meaning of an utterance requires extensive inferences on the part of listeners. Similarly, designing an utterance to be understood by a given listener requires extensive inferences on the side of the speaker. In making these inferences, speakers and listeners rely on a set of tacit assumptions that govern the conduct of conversation in everyday life. In their most widely known form, these assumptions have been expressed as four maxims by Grice (1975), a philosopher of language. Subsequent researchers have elaborated on these assumptions, specifying their implications for speakers and listeners (see Clark & Brennan, 1991; Clark &

Schober, 1992; Higgins, 1981; Higgins, Fondacaro, & McCann, 1982; Levinson, 1983; Sperber & Wilson, 1981, 1986).

CONVERSATIONAL IMPLICATIONS AND THE LOGIC OF CONVERSATION

Grice introduced his ideas on the logic of conversation in his William James lectures delivered at Harvard University in 1967. The text of these lectures has only been published in part (Grice, 1975, 1978) and his proposals were "relatively brief and only suggestive of how future work might proceed," as Levinson (1983, p. 100) noted. At present, Levinson provides the most detailed published treatment of Grice's theorizing.

The Cooperative Principle

Grice suggested that conversations are guided by a set of tacit assumptions that can be expressed in the form of four maxims which jointly express a general *cooperative principle* of conversation. Table 2.1, adapted from Levinson's (1983) discussion, summarizes these maxims.

A *maxim of manner* asks speakers to make their contribution such that it can be understood by their audience. To do so, speakers do not only need to avoid ambiguity and wordiness, but have to take the characteristics of their audience into account, designing their utterance in a way that the audience can figure out what they mean—and speakers are reasonably good at doing so (Krauss & Fussel, 1991). At the heart of this process are speakers' assumptions about the information that they share with recipients, that is, the *common ground* (Schiffer, 1972; Stalnaker, 1978). Listeners, in turn, assume that the speaker observes this maxim and interpret the speaker's utterance against what they assume to constitute the common ground (e. g., Clark, Schreuder, & Buttrick, 1983; Fussel & Krauss, 1989a, 1989b). Whereas the initial assumptions about the common ground are based on the participants' assumptions about their cultural and personal background, each successful contribution to the conversation extends the common ground of the participants, reflecting that "in orderly discourse, common ground is cumulative" (Clark & Schober, 1992, p. 19).

TABLE 2.1
The Logic of Conversation

The Cooperative Principle
Make your contribution such as is required, at the stage at which it occurs, by the accepted purpose or direction of the talk exchange in which you are engaged.

Maxim of Manner
Be perspicuous, and specifically:

(i) avoid obscurity;

(ii) avoid ambiguity;

(iii) be brief;

(iv) be orderly.

Maxim of Relation
Make your contributions relevant to the ongoing exchange.

Maxim of Quantity
(i) Make your contribution as informative as is required for the current purposes of the exchange;

(ii) do not make your contribution more informative than is required.

Maxim of Quality
Try to make your contribution one that is true, specifically:

(i) do not say what you believe to be false;

(ii) do not say for which you lack evidence.

Note. Adapted from Levinson (1983). Reprinted with permission of Cambridge University Press.

This cumulative nature of the common ground reflects, in part, the operation of a *maxim of relation* that enjoins speakers to make all contributions relevant to the aims of the ongoing conversation. This maxim entitles listeners to use the context of an utterance to disambiguate its meaning by making bridging inferences, based on the assumption that all utterances pertain to a common underlying theme (Clark, 1977). Moreover, this maxim implies that speakers are unlikely to assume that a contribution to a conversation is irrelevant to its goal, unless it is marked as such. As Sperber and Wilson (1986) noted, "communicated information comes with a guarantee of relevance"(p. vi) and if in doubt, it is the listener's task to determine the intended meaning of the utterance by referring to the common ground or by asking for clarification.

In addition, a *maxim of quantity* requires speakers to make their contribution as informative as is required, but not more informative than is required. On the one hand, speakers should provide all the information that is relevant to the conversation. On the other hand, they should respect the established, or assumed, common ground by providing the information that recipients need, without reiterating information that recipients already have (Clark & Haviland, 1977; Prince, 1981). Thus, this maxim requests full provision of relevant information as well as avoidance of redundancy. Finally, a *maxim of quality* enjoins speakers not to say anything they believe to be false or lack adequate evidence for.

Table 2.2, adapted from McCann and Higgins (1992), summarizes the implications of these maxims in the form of "rules" that speakers and listeners are supposed to follow. These rules apply most directly to situations in which participants attempt to exchange information or to get things done. Obviously, conversations

TABLE 2.2
Rules of the Communication Game

Communicators should:
1. take the recipient's characteristics into account;
2. try to be understood (i.e., be coherent and comprehensible);
3. give neither too much nor too little information;
4. be relevant;
5. produce a message that is appropriate to the context and the circumstances;
6. produce a message that is appropriate to their communicative intent or purpose;
7. convey the truth as they see it;
8. assume that the recipient is trying, as muchas possible, to follow the rules of the communication game.

Recipients should:
1. take the communicator's characteristics into account;
2. determine the communicator's communicative intent or purpose;
3. take the context and circumstances into account;
4. pay attention to the message and be prepared to receive it;
5. try to understand the message;
6. provide feedback, when possible, to the communicator concerning their understanding of the message.

Note. Adapted from McCann and Higgins (1992). Reprinted by permission of Sage.

may be characterized by other goals, in which case participants may not assume that the usual conversational maxims are observed (see Higgins, Fondacaro, & McCann, 1981). This is particularly likely in situations that are not considered cooperative, either due to their antagonistic (e.g., legal cross-examination) or playful (e.g., riddles) character (Levinson, 1983). Given that this volume is concerned with conversational processes in research settings, however, the adjustments required by different conversational goals do not need further elaboration. In general, research participants are likely to perceive the research situation as a task-oriented setting in which participants attempt to exchange information as accurately as possible, thus rendering the assumptions underlying task-oriented conversations highly relevant.

In summary, according to the tacit assumptions that govern the conduct of conversation in daily life, "communicated information comes with a guarantee of relevance" (Sperber & Wilson, 1986, p. vi) and listeners are entitled to assume that the speaker tries to be informative, truthful, relevant, and clear. Moreover, listeners interpret the speakers' utterances "on the assumption that they are trying to live up to these ideals" (Clark & Clark, 1977, p. 122).

Conversational Implicatures

An obvious objection to Grice's (1975, 1978) portrait of conversational conduct is that "no one actually speaks like that the whole time," as Levinson (1983, p. 102) said. This, however, is not Grice's point. "It is not the case, he will readily admit, that people follow these guidelines to the letter. Rather, in most ordinary kinds of talk these principles are oriented to, such that when talk does not proceed according to specifications, hearers assume that, contrary to appearances, the principles are nevertheless adhered to at some deeper level" (Levinson, 1983, p. 102). This becomes obvious when we consider the inferences we are likely to draw from utterances that do, at the surface, not conform to Grice's maxims. Grice referred to these inferences as *conversational implicatures*, that is, inferences that go beyond the semantic meaning of what is being said by determining the pragmatic meaning of the utterance. A few examples, mostly taken from Levinson may illustrate this point.

Suppose A asks, "Where is Bill?" and B responds, "There's a yellow VW outside Sue's home" (Levinson, 1983, p. 102). If taken literally, B's contribution fails to answer A's question, thus violating (at least) the maxim of relation and the maxim of quantity. When reading the exchange, however, we are unlikely to consider B's contribution an inappropriate change of topic. Rather, we infer that Bill probably has a yellow VW and that the location of the yellow VW may suggest Bill is at Sue's house. These inferences, and the ease with which readers draw them, reflect the implicit assumption that B is a cooperative communicator whose contribution is relevant to A's question. As becomes evident in the chapters that follow, this assumption underlies many biases that reflect subjects' reliance on normatively irrelevant information in research situations—much as the reader inferred that the yellow VW may have some relevance for the question posed, subjects infer the presented information is relevant to their task.

Moreover, the inferences we draw from speakers' utterances often go beyond the logical truth value of the literal statement. For example, consider the statement, "Nigel has fourteen children" (Levinson, 1983, p. 106). We are likely to interpret this utterance as implying that Nigel has exactly 14 children, no more and no less. Logically, however, the statement would also hold true if Nigel had 20 children (or any other number larger than 14). We are unlikely to draw this inference, however, because if Nigel had more than fourteen children, the speaker should have said so by following the maxim of quantity ("say as much as is required"). Similarly, suppose that A asks, "How did Harry fare in court the other day?" and B answers, "He did get a fine" (Levinson, 1983, p. 106). If it later turned out that Harry got a life sentence in addition to a fine, and B knew it all along, we would certainly feel that B was misleading A by not providing all the information relevant to the situation, thereby violating the maxim of quantity. By enjoining the provision of full information the maxim of quantity adds to most utterances "a pragmatic inference to the effect that the statement presented is the strongest, and most informative, that can be made in the situation" (Levinson, 1983, p. 106). Again, this implication of the cooperative principle is often violated in research situations.

As these and numerous other examples illustrate, speakers do not always observe the maxims of conversation in making an utterance. However, listeners are likely to assume that the speaker observed the maxims nevertheless and draw inferences based on these assumptions. It is these inferences that Grice called conversational implicatures. In fact, in many situations, speakers deliberately flount the maxims of conversation trusting that recipients will arrive at the appropriate implicature. As a pertinent example, offered in Grice's William James lecture, consider a letter of reference that contains the statement, "Miss X has nice handwriting." Assuming that a candidate's handwriting is irrelevant for judging the candidate's qualification for a fellowship, we are likely to infer something else, akin to, "On a fellowship recommendation one is supposed to say only favorable things about the candidate. Well, this is the only point in Miss X favor that I know of. Ergo, this statement implies another: 'Miss X does not deserve to get the fellowship, since she has no relevant good qualities'" (Lakoff, 1975, p. 72). Although this example violated the assumption of relevance, other violations may lead to similar conclusions. Consider, for example, a concert review that reads, "Miss Singer produced a series of sounds corresponding closely to the score of an aria from Rigoletto" (Levinson, 1983, p. 112). This statement violates the maxim of manner by being obscure and lengthy rather than clear and brief and we are likely to infer "that there was in fact some considerable difference between Miss Singer's performance and those to which the term singing is usually applied" (Levinson, 1983, p. 112).

In summary, listeners interpret speakers' utterances on the basis of the assumption that the speaker is a cooperative communicator, unless they have reason to believe otherwise (e.g., because features of the situation suggest that it is not germane to cooperative conduct). If the speaker's utterance seems to violate conversational maxims at a superficial level, listeners search for interpretations that render the utterance compatible with the assumption that the speaker was nevertheless trying to be cooperative. In doing so, they draw inferences that go beyond the literal, semantic meaning of the sentences uttered.

Such inferences are, by definition, conversational implicatures, where the term *implicature* is intended to contrast with terms like *logical implication, entailment* and *logical consequence* which are generally used to refer to inferences that are derived solely from logical or semantic content. For implicatures are not semantic inferences, but rather inferences based on both the content of what has been said and some specific assumptions about the cooperative nature of ordinary verbal interaction. (Levinson, 1983, pp. 103–104)

As the following chapters illustrate, many shortcomings and biases of human judgment reflect that researchers focus solely on the logical implications of the information they provide to research participants while the research participants themselves draw on the implicatures provided by the content and the conversational context to arrive at a judgment.

THE LOGIC OF CONVERSATIONS IN RESEARCH SETTINGS

The key hypothesis of this volume holds that research participants bring the tacit assumptions that govern the conduct of daily life to the research situation. In fact, one may argue that subjects in psychological experiments and respondents in survey interviews are forced to rely on these assumptions to a larger degree than most communicators in daily life. As many researchers have noted (e.g., Clark & Schober, 1992; Strack, 1994a, 1994b; Strack & Schwarz, 1992), "conversations" in research settings differ from natural conversations by being highly constrained. Whereas speakers and addressees collaborate in unconstrained natural conversations "to establish intended word meanings, intended interpretations of full utterances, implications of utterances, mutually recognized purposes, and many other such things" (Clark & Schober, 1992, p. 25), their opportunity to do so is severely limited in research settings, due to the researcher's attempt to standardize the interaction. Most importantly, the standardization of instructions, or of the questions asked, precludes that the utterances can be tailored to meet different common grounds. Moreover, when research participants ask for clarification, they may often not receive additional information. Rather, the previously given instructions may be repeated or a well-trained survey interviewer may respond, "Whatever it means to you," when asked to clarify a question's meaning. In some cases, as when a respondent is asked to complete a self-administered questionnaire, there may also be nobody who can be asked for clarification. As a result, a mutual negotiation of intended meaning is largely precluded in many research situations.

Nevertheless, research participants will attempt to cooperate by determining the intended meaning of the researcher's contributions to the constrained conversation. To do so, they will rely even more on the tacit assumptions that govern the conduct of conversation in daily life than they would under less constrained conditions—and these assumptions grant them every right to do so. That communicators are supposed to design their utterances such that they will be understood by addressees implies an *interpretability presumption,* as Clark and Schober (1992) noted. This presumption is emphasized by the fact that the researcher as communicator obviously does not foresee any difficulties with the comprehensibility of his or her utterances, or else he or she would have taken appropriate precautions. As a result, research participants will refer to the conversational maxims in inferring the researcher's intended meaning. Hence, they will assume that every contribution of the researcher is relevant to the aims of the ongoing conversation; that every contribution is informative, truthful, and clear; and they will refer to the context of the conversation to resolve any ambiguities that may arise.

Unfortunately, however, research participants are bound to miss a crucial difference between the research conversation and conversations in daily life. Whereas the researcher is likely to comply with conversational maxims in most conversations outside the research setting, he or she is much less likely to do so in the research setting itself. In many cases, the researcher may deliberately provide information that is neither relevant, nor truthful, informative and clear—and may have carefully designed the situation to suggest otherwise. Research participants, however, have no reason to suspect that the researcher is not a cooperative communicator. Accordingly, they try to determine the "deeper" meaning of the researcher's utterances and draw on the conversational implicatures in addition to the semantic information provided to them. The researcher, however, will evaluate their judgments against a normative model that draws solely on the semantic implications of the provided information. Any deviations from the normative model are then attributed to "faulty reasoning," although they may, at least in part, reflect "faulty communication."

The following chapters explore the extent to which conversational processes contribute to judgmental biases and shortcomings. These chapters elaborate on two central implications of a Gricean analysis of research communication.

First, communicated information comes with a guarantee of relevance and research participants draw on the cooperativeness assumption in interpreting the researcher's contributions. As a result, information that the researcher considers irrelevant by focusing on its semantic meaning is nevertheless relevant in the eyes of research participants, who focus on its pragmatic implications. The research reviewed in chapters 3 and 4 demonstrates that subjects' in psychological experiments will only rely on semantically irrelevant information when they can assume that the experimenter is a cooperative communicator. When this assumption is called into question, many well-known biases are either attenuated or eliminated. Chapter 5 extends this analysis from psychological experimentation to survey interviews, focusing on the information conveyed by formal features of questionnaires.

Second, research participants design their own contributions in compliance with conversational norms. They rely on the context of the research conversation to determine which information the researcher is interested in and tailor their answers to provide this information without reiterating information that the researcher already has or may take for granted anyway. As a result, conversational norms influence question interpretation as well as the use and disuse of information, giving raise to a variety of context effects in judgment, discussed in chapter 6.

3

The Conversational Relevance
of "Irrelevant" Information

One of the key assumptions underlying the conduct of conversation holds that all information contributed by participants is relevant to the goal of the ongoing conversation. As noted in chapter 2, research participants have no reason to assume that this maxim of relevance does not hold in a formal research setting. Accordingly, they assume that all information offered to them by the researcher is relevant to their task—and try to make sense of it. This implicit guarantee of relevance contributes in important ways to several pervasive biases that have been documented in judgment research, as this and the next chapter illustrate. Moreover, the same processes underlie many apparent "artifacts" in attitude and opinion measurement that have captured the attention of survey methodologists, addressed in chapter 5.

IF THE EXPERIMENTER PRESENTS IT, I SHOULD USE IT

Social psychologists have long been intrigued by subjects' readiness to rely on individuating information of little diagnostic value at the expense of more diagnostic information. The two most prominent examples of this general bias are the neglect of information about situational factors in explaining the behavior of an actor and the underutilization of base-rate information. As most robust phenomena, both of these biases are likely to have many determinants. Several studies indicate, however, that the conversational guarantee of relevance contributes to a considerable degree to the size of the obtained effects.

THE UNDERUTILIZATION OF BASE-RATE INFORMATION

Numerous studies have demonstrated a pronounced bias to rely on individuating information of little diagnostic value at the expense of more diagnostic base-rate information (see Nisbett & Ross, 1980, for a review). Although the initial conclusion that individuating information will typically overwhelm the impact of base-rate information (e.g., Kahneman & Tversky, 1973; Nisbett & Borgida, 1975) has been called into question by subsequent studies (see Ginossar & Trope, 1987, for a review), the frequently observed underutilization of base-rate information has continued to be a key topic in judgment and decision research. An analysis of the experimental procedures used indicates, however, that the often dramatic findings are, in part, a function of conversational processes rather than of features naturally inherent to base-rate or individuating information.

In what is probably the best-known demonstration of base-rate neglect, Kahneman and Tversky (1973) presented their subjects with the following person description:

> Jack is a 45-year-old man. He is married and has four children. He is generally conservative, careful, and ambitious. He shows no interest in political and social issues and spends most of his free time on his many hobbies, which include home carpentry, sailing, and mathematical puzzles.

Based on this description, subjects predicted that the target person is most likely an engineer, independently of whether the base-rate probability for any target being an engineer was .30 or .70. This reflects that subjects based their judgment on the similarity between the described person and their stereotype of a typical engineer. In doing so, they relied on a *representativeness heuristic*, according to which probability judgments are based on "the degree of correspondence between a sample and a population, an instance and a category, an act and an actor, or, more generally, between an outcome and a model" (Tversky & Kahneman, 1983, p. 295). Relying on this heuristic, subjects largely ignored the base-rate information provided to them, in contrast to what normative models of probability judgment would want them to do. Did subjects not understand that the a priori likelihood of any target being an

engineer is relevant to their task? And did they fail to notice that
the person description is of little diagnostic value?

An analysis of the instructions used in Kahneman and Tversky's
(1973) study proves informative. Specifically, the instructions read
(italics added):

> A panel of *psychologists* have *interviewed* and administered *person-
> ality tests* to 30 (resp., 70) engineers and 70 (resp. 30) lawyers, all
> successful in their respective fields. On the basis of *this* information,
> thumbnail descriptions of the 30 engineers and 70 lawyers have
> been written. You will find on your forms five descriptions, chosen
> at random from the 100 available descriptions. For each description,
> please indicate your probability that the person described is an
> engineer, on a scale from 0 to 100.

> The same task has been performed by a panel of *experts* who were
> *highly accurate* in assigning probabilities to the various descrip-
> tions. You will be paid a bonus to the extent that your estimates come
> close to those of the expert panel.

The first part of these instructions informs subjects that the
individuating information was compiled by psychologists on the
basis of respected procedures of their profession, namely interviews and tests. Given that laypersons assume psychologists to be
experts on issues of personality (rather than base rates), this introduction emphasizes the relevance of the individuating information.
Moreover, other experts—most likely psychologists as well, given
the present context—are said to be highly accurate in making these
judgments, thus further increasing the relevance of the individuating information. The subjects' task is then defined as determining
a probability that matches the judgments of the experts. If these
experts are assumed to be psychologists, subjects can infer that the
experimenter wants them to use the same information that these
experts used—which is most likely the personality information
compiled by their colleagues.

Finally, as the experiment proceeds, subjects are asked to judge
several target persons for whom different individuating information is presented. The base-rate information about the sample from
which the targets are drawn, on the other hand, is held constant.
This further suggests that the individuating information is of crucial
importance because this information provides different clues for
each judgment and in the absence of this information all tasks

would have the same solution. Thus, the instructions and proce-dures of Kahneman and Tversky's classic study allowed subjects to infer (however incorrectly) the experimenter's intention that they should base their judgment on the individuating information. It therefore comes as little surprise that subjects relied on it when making their judgments. After all, they had no reason to assume that the experimenter violated each and every of the Gricean maxims by providing information that is neither relevant, nor truthful, informative, and clear.

Undermining Conversational Relevance

This conversational analysis suggests that subjects' reliance on individuating personality information should be greatly attenuated when the experimenter's intention to communicate the relevance of this information cannot be inferred from the social context of the experimental situation, that is when the usual rules of social dis-course are suspended. A similar effect should be obtained if the task is framed such that the source of the individuating information, and the experts who provide accurate predictions, are not experts on individuating information (like psychologists) but experts on base-rate information (like statisticians).

To test these hypotheses, Schwarz, Strack, Hilton, and Naderer (1991, Experiment 1) conducted a modified partial replication of Kahneman and Tversky's study. Subjects received a German trans-lation of the original person description presented earlier and were informed that this person was randomly selected from a sample of 30 engineers and 70 lawyers. Let us first consider the conditions in which the task was framed as a psychology problem. In these conditions, some subjects were told that the person description was written by a psychologist, replicating the instructions used by Kahneman and Tversky. This entitles the recipient to assume that the presented information obeys the normative rules of communi-cation and reflects a particular communicative intention on the part of the experimenter. Other subjects were told that the (identical) description was compiled by a computer that drew a random sample of descriptive sentences bearing on the target person. Obviously, the cooperative principle does not directly apply to the resulting communication and the communicative intention cannot be unam-biguously inferred. Facing what is said to be a random sample drawn from a pool of expert statements, subjects may question the usefulness of the selection, in particular when the information presented is of little informational value. Thus, they may be less likely to "make sense" of this information than when it were presented as a narrative by a psychologist, who presumably tried to be informative and relevant. Therefore, they should rely less on the individuating information when it was drawn by a computer rather than presented as a narrative written by a psychologist.

The results confirmed this prediction, as shown in the first row of Table 3.1. Replicating Kahneman and Tversky's (1973) findings, subjects who received the individuating information as a narrative written by a psychologist estimated the likelihood of the target being an engineer as .76, despite a low base rate of .30. However, when the same information was allegedly selected by a computer, their likelihood estimate dropped to .40. This significant attenuation indicates that subjects' reliance on individuating information at the expense of base-rate information reflects, in part, their assumption that the experimenter is a cooperative communicator who does not present information that is irrelevant to the task at hand. Accordingly, they tried to find "relevance" in the information provided to them, unless the implicit guarantee of relevance was called into question. Consistent with this notion, subjects in the computer-generated description condition were more likely to complain that they received "useless" information when asked during a postexperimental debriefing.

In another set of conditions, shown in the second row of Table 3.1, the same task was framed as a statistics problem. In this case, unspecified researchers were said to have compiled the descriptive

TABLE 3.1
**Estimated Probability of Target Being an Engineer
as a Function of Conversational Context**

	Individuating Information	
Framing	Written by Researcher	Compiled by Computer
Psychology problem	.76	.40
Statistics problem	.55	.74

Note. N is 11 per cell. The base-rate probability is .30. Adapted from Schwarz, Strack, Hilton, and Naderer (1991, Experiment 1). Reprinted by permission.

information about the target and statisticians were said to be the experts who do well at solving the task. This frame should render individuating information less relevant, reflecting that statisticians are experts on base rates rather than on personality. Confirming this prediction, subjects relied less on narrative individuating information when the task was presented as a statistics problem, resulting in a mean likelihood estimate of .55, than when it was presented as a psychology problem. This finding confirms Zukier and Pepitone's (1984) previous observation of framing effects. In their study, subjects relied less on individuating information when they were asked to make their judgment like "a scientist analyzing data" than when the task was introduced as pertaining to "clinical judgments." In the latter condition, subjects were explicitly asked to call on their "general knowledge, sensitivity, and empathy" in understanding "the individual's personality, profession, inclinations and interests" (p. 353), resulting in increased reliance on the individuating information.

More importantly, however, it is conceivable that the framing of the task as a psychology or a statistics problem may change the meaning of the source manipulation introduced in Schwarz, Strack, Hilton, and Naderer's (1991) study. Random sampling is a valued statistical procedure that is assumed to result in a representative representation of the population from which the sample is drawn. To the extent that the framing of the task as a statistics problem activates this concept of *random sampling*, subjects may consider a random sample of descriptive sentences a stochastic event that results in a description that is more representative of the target's behavior than a thumbnail description provided by an unspecified researcher, whose particular expertise on personality issues is unknown. If so, they may rely more on what is purportedly a "representative" sample of descriptive information, resulting in a more pronounced impact of the individuating information under "random sampling" conditions. Again, the results confirmed this prediction, as shown in the second row of Table 3.1. Specifically, subjects provided a mean likelihood estimate of .74 under this condition, thus giving more weight to the individuating information when it was presented as a random sample drawn by a computer rather than a narrative written by an unspecified "researcher."

In combination, these findings indicate that subjects considered the context of the experiment to infer which information is particularly relevant to their task. Accordingly, they were more likely to rely on individuating information of low diagnosticity at the expense of base-rate information when the individuating information was provided by an expert on personality rather than a nonspecified researcher. In addition, their use of individuating information depended on the framing of the task and the alleged source. When the task was framed as a psychology problem, subjects relied more on personality information when it was selected by a human communicator, who they could assume to comply to conversational norms, than when it was selected by a computer. In contrast, they relied more on a random sample of descriptive information drawn by a computer when the framing of the task as a statistics problem matched that presentation style, presumably implying representativeness of the randomly sampled information. Thus, their use of different sources of information reflected reasonable inferences about their respective relevance, based on the specific context in which the information was presented.

This conclusion is consistent with previous research that demonstrated that base-rate information is likely to be used when it is highly relevant to the task at hand and its relevance is apparent in the respective context (see Ginossar & Trope, 1987; Higgins & Bargh, 1987; Trope & Ginossar, 1988, for reviews). Whereas this research focused on explicit task characteristics, the present study indicates that subjects' inferences about the nature of their task and the relevance of the presented information depend on the specifics of the communicative context. Where their judgments deviated most clearly from normative models, they did so because subjects went beyond the literal meaning of the information given and used the communicative context to determine the nature of the task and the relevance of the various sources of information.

Constant Versus Variable Base-Rates: The Problems of Within-Subjects Designs

In many base-rate studies, the apparent relevance of individuating information is further enhanced by the use of a within-subjects design. For example, in Kahneman and Tversky's (1973) study, subjects received descriptions of five different persons who were all said to be drawn from the same sample. Thus, the individuating information was varied while the base rate was held constant. If subjects use the experimental context to determine the exact nature of their task, this procedure implicitly suggests that the judgment should be based on those aspects of the information that varies over the course of the experiment. This "variation principle" presumably indicates that the experimenter is interested in how well subjects can discriminate between persons who are differentially likely to be lawyers or engineers. This interpretation may be particularly suitable because the task would otherwise result in identical solutions for each of the five targets drawn from the same sample, and it may be hard to see why "experts" (and most notably, psychologists) are needed to do well.

A reversal of the procedure emphasizes this point. Suppose that subjects are provided with the description of a single person and are asked to estimate the probability that this person is an engineer (a) if drawn from a sample of 10 engineers and 90 lawyers, or (b) if drawn from a sample of 30 engineers and 70 lawyers. It seems likely that subjects would construe their task as pertaining to the impact of base rates on the likelihood of the target person being an engineer, and, accordingly, would utilize the base-rate information presented to them. This thought experiment suggests that the use of information does not depend on its diagnosticity per se but on subjects' perception of the experimenter's communicative intention, which is inferred from the instructions and the context of the task. Based on the inferred intention, subjects determine the nature of their task and draw on the information that seems most relevant.

Several studies confirmed this hypothesis (e.g., Fischhoff, Slovic, & Lichtenstein, 1979; Schwarz, Strack, Hilton, & Naderer, 1991, Experiment 2). For example, Schwarz and colleagues varied either the individuating or the base-rate information within subjects. In addition, they framed the task either as a psychology problem or as a statistics problem, as previously described. In all conditions, the individuating information was presented as a narrative written by a human communicator, who was said to be a psychologist (in the psychology framing condition) or an unspecified "researcher" (in the statistics framing condition). Table 3.2 shows the results.

Overall, subjects gave more weight to the individuating information when the task was framed as a psychology problem rather than a statistics problem, replicating the results discussed earlier.

TABLE 3.2
Estimated Probability of Target Being an Engineer
as a Function of Framing and Within Subjects Variation

Framing	Within-Subjects Variation			
	One Person, One Sample	Two Persons, One Sample	One Person, Two Samples	
Psychology	.69	.82	.55	.69
Statistics	.56	.65	.48	.56
	.62	.73	.51	

Note. *N* is 8 per cell. The base-rate probability is .30. Adapted from Schwarz, Strack, Hilton, and Naderer (1991, Experiment 2). Reprinted by permission.

More importantly, the impact of individuating and base-rate information depended on which information was varied within subjects. When a single target person was described as showing no interest in political issues and enjoying home carpentry and mathematical puzzles, subjects estimated the likelihood of the target being an engineer as . 62, despite a low base-rate probability of .30 for any target being an engineer. When the description of this target person was preceded by the description of another person drawn from the same sample, their likelihood estimate increased significantly to .73, reflecting that they gave more weight to the individuating information when it was varied within subjects. In contrast, they gave more weight to the base-rate information when this information was varied within subjects. Under this condition, subjects first had to estimate the likelihood that the target is an engineer when drawn from a sample of 10 engineers and 90 lawyers. Next, they had to estimate the likelihood that the same target is an engineer when drawn from a sample of 30 engineers and 70 lawyers. In this case, their likelihood estimate dropped significantly to .51. Although this latter estimate still reflects an underutilization of base-rate information, the overall pattern of results indicates that subjects' relative reliance on individuating and base-rate information varied as a function of their inferences about the nature of their task: When the base-rate information remains the same, whereas the individuating information varies, subjects assume that the experimenter is interested in how well they can discriminate between the different individuals described to them, rendering the individuating information particularly relevant.

Presentation Order and Inferred Relevance

In the studies just discussed, subjects were more likely to rely on individuating information of low diagnosticity when the nature of the source (human communicator vs. computer) or of their task (within subjects variation) rendered it relevant. Extending this theme, Krosnick, Li, and Lehman (1990) observed that the impact of individuating information varied as a function of the order in which the individuating and the base-rate information were presented. In seven studies, using a variety of different problems, subjects were more likely to use base-rate information when this information was presented after rather than before the individuating information. At first glance, such a recency effect may suggest that the information presented last was more accessible in memory. However, recall data and other manipulations rendered this interpretation implausible (see Krosnick et al., 1990). Rather, the emergence of this recency effect could be traced to the operation of conversational conventions.

As Krosnick et al. (1990) suggested, subjects who first receive base-rate information and are subsequently provided with individuating information may reason, "The first piece of information I was given (i. e., the base-rate) has clear implications for my judgment, so it was sufficient. A speaker should only give me additional information if it is highly relevant and informative, so the experimenter must believe that the individuating information should be given special weight in my judgment" (p. 141). This reasoning would not only imply the general guarantee of relevance addressed,but would also reflect the conversational convention to present the more informative and important information later in an utterance, in part to direct listeners' attention to it (see Clark, 1985). In turn, listeners may assume that "information presented later is more important and should be the focus of their attention" (Krosnick et al., 1990, p. 1141). If so, the individuating information may be rendered particularly relevant in the conversational context if presented after rather than before the base-rate information.

Several findings support this assumption. In one of their studies, Krosnick et al. (1990, Experiment 4) observed that base-rate information had a more pronounced impact when the base rate was presented after rather than before the individuating information. However, this recency effect was largely eliminated when subjects were informed that the order in which both pieces of information were presented was determined at random. Thus, subjects were likely to rely on the information presented last, unless the informational value of presentation order was called into question. Moreover, this order effect only emerged when the base-rate information contradicted the implications of the individuating information. In this case, subjects gave more weight to whatever information was presented last, suggesting that the presentation order may carry information about the relative importance that the communicator wants to convey.

To provide direct evidence for this assumption, Krosnick et al. (1990, Experiment 7) asked subjects to complete the blanks in a transcript of a conversation concerned with buying a car. In the base rate-last condition, the crucial part of this transcript read,

> My brother-in-law has had one problem after another with his Saab. _____ a car magazine survey found Saabs have a better repair record than Volvos. Considering all this, I decided to buy a _____. I think that is the better choice.

In contrast, in the base-rate first condition the transcript read,

> A car magazine survey found Saabs have a better repair record than Volvos. _____ my brother-in-law has had one problem after another with his Saab. Considering all this, I decided to buy a _____. I think that is the better choice.

As expected on the basis of conversational conventions, most subjects completed the blanks in a way that implied that the speaker considered the second piece of information as more relevant than the first piece. Moreover, most of these subjects assumed that the speaker decided to buy the car favored by the second piece of information.

Conclusions

In combination, the findings of the Schwarz, Strack, Hilton, and Naderer (1991) and Krosnick et al. (1990) studies indicate that subjects based their judgment primarily on the information that corresponded to the inferred communicative intention of the communicator. In the psychology framing conditions of the

Schwarz, Strack, Hilton, and Naderer (1991) study, subjects were more likely to rely on the individuating information if it was presented by a human communicator, who they could expect to comply with conversational norms, rather than drawn by a computer. Similarly, in the Krosnick et al. (1990) studies, subjects gave differential weight to base-rate and to individuating information depending on its apparent importance to the communicator, as conveyed by the presentation order chosen. In both cases, it was not the nature of the presented information per se that determined its impact, but rather its perceived relevance in a given conversational context. The same theme is echoed in research on another well-known judgmental bias, namely the fundamental attribution error.

THE FUNDAMENTAL ATTRIBUTION ERROR

Numerous studies in the domain of person perception have documented a pronounced readiness to account for an actor's behavior in terms of his or her dispositions, even under conditions where the actor has responded to obvious situational pressures (see Jones, 1990; Ross & Nisbett, 1991, for reviews). Following a classic study by Jones and Harris (1967), this so-called correspondence bias (Jones, 1990) or fundamental attribution error (Ross, 1977) is typically investigated in an attitude–attribution paradigm. In most studies, subjects are provided an essay that advocates a certain position and are asked to infer the author's attitude. Depending on the experimental condition, they are either informed that the position taken in the essay was freely chosen by the author or was assigned by the experimenter. Whereas the content of the essay is presumably diagnostic for the author's attitude under free-choice conditions, it is not under assignment conditions. Nevertheless, subjects typically attribute attitudes to the author that reflect the position taken in the essay, even under conditions where this position was assigned.

Whereas findings of this type are usually interpreted as evidence for a pervasive "dispositional bias," subjects seem quite aware that the essay is of little diagnostic value under no-choice conditions. For example, Miller, Schmidt, Meyer, and Colella (1984) observed that a majority of their subjects explicitly reported that the essay written under no-choice conditions did not provide useful information about the author's true attitude. Nevertheless, the same subjects proceeded to make attitude attributions in line with the assigned position advocated in the essay. As Wright and Wells (1988) suggested, a violation of conversational norms on the side of the experimenter seems to contribute to this finding. Specifically, Wright and Wells (1988) noted that "the direction and content of the essay in the critical no-choice condition are irrelevant to the correct solution of the attribution task because the external constraints are sufficient to account for the essayist's behavior"(p. 184). The experimenter nevertheless provides subjects with an essay, thus violating the maxim of relevance. However, subjects have no reason to expect that this maxim is violated and are thus likely to assume "that the experimenter believes that the essay has some diagnostic value (otherwise, why were they given the essay?)" (p. 184). Accordingly, they take the essay into consideration in making attitude attributions, resulting in an apparent dispositional bias.

To test this conversational account, Wright and Wells conducted an attitude–attribution study in which subjects were exposed to a pro or a con essay, allegedly written under choice or no-choice conditions. However, in addition to the standard procedure, their study involved a condition designed to undermine the implicit guarantee of relevance. Subjects in this condition were told that "the information packages and questionnaire items being given to subjects (. . .) were being randomly selected from a larger pool of information packages and questions. Thus, their pool might not include sufficient information for them to answer some of their questions. Moreover, their information package might contain some information that was not germane to some of their questions" (Wright & Wells, 1988, p. 185).

This manipulation significantly reduced the emerging dispositional bias relative to the standard conditions in which subjects could assume that all the information provided to them is relevant to the task at hand, as shown in Table 3.3. When the standard procedures were used, the attitudes that subjects attributed to the authors of the pro and con essays differed by 3.6 scale points on a 9-point scale, despite the fact that the authors had no choice which position to advocate. The modified procedures described here reduced this difference to 1.7 scale points, thus cutting the otherwise observed bias to less than half its size. Moreover, the impact of undermining the guarantee of relevance was limited to the theoretically relevant no-choice conditions, and the manipulation

TABLE 3.3
The Fundamental Attribution Error: Mean Attributions of Attitudes

	Standard Procedures	Modified Procedures
No choice		
pro essay	6.3	5.8
con essay	2.7	4.1
Choice		
pro essay	7.6	8.1
con essay	1.9	1.2

Note. $N = 192$. Higher numbers indicate more favorable attributed attitudes on a 9-point scale. Adapted from Wright and Wells (1988). Reprinted by permission.

did not affect subjects' inferences from essays written under free choice. Hence, undermining the guarantee of relevance did not result in generally more cautious judgments. Rather, it set subjects free to rely on the information that they themselves considered diagnostic, without having to find "relevance" in the information provided by the experimenter.

CONCLUSIONS

As the reviewed studies indicate, some of the more dramatic demonstrations of judgmental biases in social cognition research may be less likely to reflect genuine shortcomings of the judgmental process than has typically been assumed. In fact, subjects often seem quite aware that the normatively irrelevant information is, indeed, of little informational value. Nevertheless, they typically proceed to use it in making a judgment. As the studies discussed here suggest, however, this may often reflect a violation of conversational norms by the experimenter, rather than any inherently flawed reasoning by subjects. Subjects have no reason to assume that the experimenter would intentionally provide information that is uninformative and irrelevant to the task at hand, thus violating the tacit rules that govern the conduct of conversation in everyday life. Accordingly, they proceed on the basis of the assumption that the experimenter is a cooperative communicator and try to make sense of the information provided to them. Once the implicit guarantee of relevance is called into question, however, the impact of normatively irrelevant information is largely reduced. The errors that subjects commit by relying on the conversational relevance of normatively irrelevant information are unlikely to result in mistakes in everyday contexts where communicators try conform to conversational norms, provide information that is relevant to the judgment at hand, and make the task one that is clear rather than ambiguous—and where recipients are indeed expected to use contextual cues to disambiguate the communication, should the communicator not live up to the standard. As Funder (1987) noted in a related context, "it seems ironic that going beyond the information given in this way is so often interpreted by social psychologists as symptomatic of flawed judgment. Current thinking in the field of artificial intelligence is that this propensity is exactly what makes people smarter than computers"(p. 82).

This analysis suggests that some of the more frequently used procedures in social cognition research are likely to result in an overestimation of the size and the pervasiveness of judgmental biases relative to what we may expect in daily life. I emphasize, however, that this analysis does not imply that violations of conversational norms are the *sole* source of judgmental biases. Like most robust phenomena, judgmental biases are likely to be overdetermined. In fact, underutilization of base rates as well as dispositionalism in causal attribution have been observed in settings that do not involve violations of conversational norms (see Kahneman & Lavallo, 1993; Ross, 1977, for examples). Nevertheless, if we are to understand the underlying cognitive processes, we need to ensure that the emergence and size of the relevant phenomena in our experiments does not reflect the operation of determinants that are unlikely to hold in natural settings.

4

Questions, Innuendos, and Assertions of the Obvious

Whereas the research examples reviewed in chapter 3 pertained to the impact of explicit assertions of little informational value, the questions a researcher asks may also constitute a powerful source of bias. Their impact can be traced to recipients' assumption that the questioner is a cooperative communicator, which renders the presuppositions conveyed by the question relevant to the task at hand.

INFERRING A RELEVANT BACKGROUND

Questions come with the same guarantee of relevance as any other utterance. When a questioner asks, "Did you see the children getting on the school bus?" (Loftus, 1975, p. 568) he or she implies that there was a school bus in the first place or else the presupposition would violate the maxims of conversation. In other cases, the question does not entail an assertion, but based on the maxim of relevance we may infer that there is a background that renders the question relevant. Hence, asking, "Is Jane taking drugs?" suggests there may be some reason to believe she is (Wegner, Wenzlaff, Kerker, & Beattie, 1981). As the studies reviewed in this chapter illustrate, however, the biasing effects of questions are again mediated by researchers' violations of conversational norms and respondents' erroneous assumption that the questioner is a cooperative communicator.

Making Sense of Ambiguous Questions: The Case of Fictitious Issues

To begin with an extreme example, consider questions about issues that do not exist. Public opinion researchers have long been concerned that the "fear of appearing uninformed" may induce "many respondents to conjure up opinions even when they had not given the particular issue any thought prior to the interview" (Erikson, Luttberg, & Tedin, 1988, p. 44). To explore how meaningful respondents' answers are, survey researchers introduced questions about highly obscure or even completely fictitious issues, such as the "Agricultural Trade Act of 1978" (e.g., Bishop, Oldendick, & Tuchfarber 1986; Schuman & Presser, 1981). Presumably, respondents' willingness to report an opinion on a fictitious issue casts some doubt on the reports provided in survey interviews in general. In fact, about 30% of the respondents do typically provide an answer to issues that are invented by the researcher. This has been interpreted as evidence for the operation of social pressure that induces respondents to give answers, which are presumably based on a "mental flip of coin" (Converse, 1964, 1970). Rather than providing a meaningful opinion, respondents are assumed to generate some random response, apparently confirming social scientists' wildest nightmares.

From a conversational point of view, however, these responses may be more meaningful than has typically been assumed in public opinion research. From this point of view, the sheer fact that a question about some issue is asked presupposes that this issue exists—or else asking a question about it would violate the norms of cooperative conduct. Respondents, however, have no reason to assume that the researcher would ask meaningless questions and will hence try to make sense of it (see Strack & Martin, 1987; Sudman, Bradburn, & Schwarz, 1996, chapter 3; Tourangeau, 1984, for general discussions of respondents' tasks). If the question is highly ambiguous, and the interviewer does not provide additional clarification, respondents are likely to turn to the context of the ambiguous question to determine its meaning, much as they would be expected to do in any other conversation. Once respondents have assigned a particular meaning to the issue, thus transforming the fictitious issue into a better defined issue that makes sense in the context of the interview, they may have no difficulty in reporting a subjectively meaningful opinion. Even if they have not given the particular issue much thought, they may easily identify the broader set of issues to which this particular one apparently belongs. If so, they can use their general attitude toward the broader set of issues to determine their attitude toward this particular one.

A study by Strack, Schwarz, and Wänke (1991, Experiment 1) illustrates this point. In this study, German college students were asked to report their attitudes toward an "educational contribution." For some subjects, this target question was preceded by a question that asked them to estimate the average tuition fees that students have to pay at U.S. universities (in contrast to Germany, where university education is free). Others had to estimate the amount of money that the Swedish government pays every student as financial support. As expected, students supported the introduction of an educational contribution when the preceding question referred to money that students receive from the government, but opposed it when the preceding question referred to tuition fees. Subsequently, respondents were asked what the educational contribution implied. Content analyses of respondents' definitions of the fictitious issue clearly demonstrated that respondents used the context of the educational contribution question to determine its meaning.

Thus, respondents turned to the content of related questions to determine the meaning of an ambiguous one. In doing so, they interpreted the ambiguous question in a way that made sense of it, and subsequently provided a subjectively meaningful response to their definition of the question. Accordingly, it comes as no surprise that responses to fictitious issues do not conform to a model of mental coin flipping as Converse and other early researchers hypothesized. Rather, they show a meaningful pattern that is systematically related to respondents' attitudes in substantively related domains (e.g., Schwarz, Strack, Hippler, & Bishop, 1991; see also Schuman & Kalton, 1985). What is at the heart of reported opinions about fictitious issues is not that respondents are willing to give subjectively meaningless answers, but that researchers violate conversational rules by asking meaningless questions in a context that suggests otherwise. And much as has been observed in response to useless information presented in psychological experiments, survey respondents work hard at finding meaning in the questions asked. The same theme is echoed in psychological research into the role of leading questions on eyewitness testimony and the impact of innuendos in impression formation.

Leading Questions in Eyewitness Research

In a highly influential program of research, Loftus and collaborators (e.g., Loftus, 1975; see Loftus, 1979, for a review) demonstrated a pronounced impact of the presuppositions conveyed by leading questions on subjects' memory. In a typical study, subjects are shown a brief film clip and subsequently have to answer questions about what they saw. For some subjects, these questions include references to objects or events that were not presented. For example, Loftus (1975, Experiment 4) asked subjects, "Did you see the children getting on the school bus?" although no school bus was shown in the film. One week later, these subjects were more likely to erroneously remember having seen the school bus presupposed in the leading question than subjects who were not exposed to the question. Findings of this type have typically been interpreted as indicating that "a presupposition of unknown truthfulness will likely be treated as fact, incorporated into memory, and subsequently 'known' to be true" (Dodd & Bradshaw, 1980, p. 695).

Not surprisingly, such biasing effects of leading questions received considerable attention in applied research into eyewitness testimony. Several studies suggest, however, that the applied implications of this line of work may be more limited than has been assumed. In most experiments, the leading question is asked by the experimenter and subjects have no reason to assume that the experimenter may lead them astray by knowingly introducing unwarranted presuppositions, thus violating conversational norms. In an actual courtroom setting, on the other hand, people may be quite aware that communicators may follow their own agenda, may be motivated to introduce misleading information, and may not be cooperative. Hence, the impact of leading questions may be restricted to conditions under which the questioner is assumed to be a cooperative communicator.

In line with this assumption, Dodd and Bradshaw (1980) observed biasing effects of leading questions about an observed car accident when the source of the question was the researcher, but not when the source was said to be the defendant's lawyer (Experiment 1) or the driver of the car who caused the accident (Experiment 2). For example, subjects in the experimental conditions of their first study were asked four misleading questions. Two days later, control group subjects, who were not exposed to misleading questions, falsely remembered having seen .43 of the four presupposed objects. For subjects who were exposed to misleading questions from an unspecified source, the false recognition increased to .94 out of four objects. If the misleading questions were attributed to the "lawyer representing the driver of the car causing the accident" (Dodd & Bradshaw, 1980, p. 697), however, the misleading questions had no significant impact. In this case, subjects' erroneous recognition of .53 objects resembled the errors made under control conditions, where no misleading questions were introduced to begin with. Thus, the otherwise obtained biasing effects of leading questions were "canceled by attributing the verbal material to a source that may be presumed to be biased" (Dodd & Bradshaw, 1980, p. 701), calling the source's cooperativeness into question. Similarly, V. Smith and Ellsworth (1987) only obtained a biasing effect of leading questions when the questioner was assumed to be highly familiar with the event that the subject had witnessed. When the questioner was assumed to be unfamiliar with the event, the presupposition was discounted and no impact of the leading question was obtained.

As these results indicate, "presuppositions are not simply and automatically accepted by recipients" (Dodd & Bradshaw, 1980, p. 699). Rather, recipients must assume that the speaker is a cooperative communicator who commands the relevant knowledge and has no intention to mislead. If either of these assumptions is called into question, the presuppositions implied by misleading questions are unlikely to lead subjects astray. Hence, misleading question effects are more likely to be obtained when the misleading questions are introduced by the experimenter, who subjects can assume to be cooperative and knowledgeable with regard to the material presented to them, than under the courtroom conditions on which the experiments are supposed to bear.

Whereas Loftus' research program focused mainly on the impact of leading questions on reconstructive memory, other researchers explored the impact of leading questions on impression formation. Their findings, again, reiterate the same theme.

Questions and Innuendos in Impression Formation

For example, in an exploration of incrimination through innuendo, Wegner et al. (1981) observed that media questions of the type, "Is Jane using drugs?" may quickly become public answers. Again, recipients infer that there must be some evidence that triggered the question in the first place—or why else would someone raise it? Here, as well as in Loftus' research program, the impact of the presupposition conveyed by the question rests on the implicit assumption that the communicator is cooperative, as a study by Swann, Giuliano, and Wegner (1982) illustrates. In their study, subjects observed how a questioner asked a respondent a leading question of the type, "What would you do to liven things up at a party?" As expected, subjects considered the question to provide conjectural evidence that the person asked is an extrovert—unless they were told that the questions had been drawn from a fishbowl, thus undermining the implicit guarantee of relevance.

ON SAYING THINGS THAT GO WITHOUT SAYING

In the examples just reviewed, respondents assumed that there is a background that legitimates the presupposition conveyed in the question—that the fictitious issue exists, that there was a school bus, or that one had reason to wonder whether Jane takes drugs. Without a proper background, the question asked would violate each and every maxim of conversational conduct. Ironically, misleading assumptions about a relevant background may not only be drawn from misleading questions but also from correct assertions—provided that the assertion asserts the obvious. As noted in chapter 2, speakers are expected to be informative, that is, to provide information that is new to the recipient, rather than information that the recipient already has or may take for granted anyway. Hence, a speaker who asserts something that "goes without saying" must have reason to believe that the assertion is informative. This is the case when there is some background that suggests that the apparently obvious may not hold in the specific case.

As an example, suppose that I tell you my friend Peter does not beat his wife. Assuming that most people do not beat their spouses, you may wonder why I am providing this information? Perhaps Peter is generally an aggressive person, who beats many people, but at least he doesn't beat his wife? Or perhaps he has many fights with his wife, but they don't involve physical violence? Or perhaps something is wrong with me and I assume beating one's wife is a normal part of life, rendering Peter's good behavior noteworthy?

In fact, each of these inferences may be drawn as Gruenfeld, Wyer, and their colleagues observed (see Wyer & Gruenfeld, 1995, for a review). Again, however, recipients' assumptions about the applicability of conversational norms is crucial.

For example, Gruenfeld and Wyer (1992) presented college students with propositions that most subjects in the population considered false to begin with. Some statements asserted the validity of the proposition (e.g., "The CIA is engaged in illegal drug trafficking"), whereas other statements denied the validity of the proposition, thus confirming what subjects believed to begin with. In one condition of their experiment, the statements were attributed to a newspaper, that is, a source supposed to provide newsworthy information. In this case, affirming as well as denying the validity of the proposition increased subjects' belief that the proposition was actually true. For example, confirming subjects' a priori belief that the CIA is not engaged in illegal drug trafficking, increased their belief that the CIA may indeed be involved in drug trafficking—or else, why would the denial be newsworthy? This inference of a background that renders an otherwise irrelevant denial informative, however, was not obtained when the statements were attributed to an encyclopedia. Encyclopedias are supposed to convey archival knowledge, which includes pieces of information that may "go without saying" for many readers. Hence, finding the obvious in an encyclopedia does not trigger inferences about a relevant background.

The same process underlies the effectiveness of many misleading advertisements (see Harris & Monaco, 1978, for a general review). Suppose, for example, that the label on a bottle of olive oil asserts that the oil is "cholesterol free." This assertion is correct and applies to all olive oils. Nevertheless, consumers assume that there must be a reason for presenting this information—and infer that other brands of olive oil are likely to contain some cholesterol (Schwarz, 1996). Hence, statements of the obvious allow advertisers to implicitly mislead about other products by asserting the truth about their own.

CONCLUSIONS

In combination, the reviewed research on answers to fictitious issues and the impact of leading questions and innuendos again highlights the crucial role of the Gricean cooperativeness principle in the conduct of research. Facing a question that pertains to an ambiguous issue, research participants draw on the context of the question to infer its meaning. And being confronted with their own poor recollection of the stimulus materials shown to them, they draw on the cues provided by the experimenter's questions. Their key mistake is that they do not expect the researcher to ask a question about an issue that doesn't exist, or to present a question that presupposes a stimulus they have not been shown. Clearly, theoretical accounts of the processes underlying answers to fictitious issues or the impact of leading questions and innuendos have to take the assumed cooperativeness of the questioner into account.

What renders a leading question "leading," for example, is not the semantic information it conveys, but the inferences recipients draw based on the assumption that the communicator is cooperative. Accordingly, leading question effects are only observed when recipients can assume that the speaker has access to the relevant knowledge and is a cooperative communicator who complies with the Gricean maxims. Only under those conditions can they expect the communicator to provide information that is informative, truthful, relevant, and clear. From this perspective, the robustness of leading question effects under laboratory conditions is not surprising: As the research reviewed in the preceding sections illustrated, subjects typically assume that the experimenter is a cooperative communicator and are hence likely to rely on the implications conveyed by the experimenter's questions. Moreover, the experimenter is presumably a particularly knowledgeable source—after all, who would be more likely to know what was presented in the stimulus materials? By the same token, however, leading questions may provide less of a problem in natural settings, in which "there is often a basis to believe that the interrogator does not know the facts and is likely to have reasons to mislead" (Dodd & Bradshaw, 1980, p. 696). Much as the examples reviewed in chapter 3, the research discussed here again suggests that we need to pay closer attention to the communicative aspects of our research procedures if we are to understand the operation of judgmental biases in natural settings.

5

The Conversational Relevance of Formal Features of Questionnaires

Much as psychologists have observed that their subjects' judgments are strongly affected by normatively irrelevant information, survey researchers have observed that respondents' answers to a survey question are often influenced by presumably "irrelevant" features of questionnaire design. For example, respondents evaluate politicians more favorably (Schwarz & Hippler, 1995), and report that they themselves had more success in life (Schwarz, Knäuper, et al., 1991), when an 11-point rating scale runs from -5 to +5, rather than from 0 to 10. Moreover, they report watching more television (Schwarz et al., 1985), or suffering from a higher frequency of physical symptoms (Schwarz & Scheuring, 1992), when they are asked to report their behavior on a scale that presents low rather than high frequency response alternatives, as the examples given here will illustrate. And when asked an opinion question, they say "don't know" when this alternative is offered to them, but are happy to report an opinion when it is not (Schuman & Presser, 1981).

Findings of this type are often considered to reflect thoughtless responding, which may be avoided if people were only smart enough or motivated enough to engage in the required cognitive effort (e.g., Krosnick, 1991). A conversational perspective, however, suggests that just the opposite may be true. Behaving as cooperative communicators, respondents may do their best to make sense of the questions asked of them, drawing on all the information provided by the researcher, which includes apparently formal features of the questionnaire. Much as they assume that every contribution of the experimenter is relevant to their task in psychological experiments, so do they assume that the response scales provided to them are meaningful components of the questionnaire. Little do they know that the scale may have been constructed haphazardly or may have been chosen to maximize technical convenience rather than substantive meaning.

THE NUMERIC VALUE OF RATINGS SCALES

As a first example, consider the presentation format of rating scales. According to measurement theory, a 7-point rating scale is a 7-point rating scale, independent of how the seven points are graphically represented in the layout of the questionnaire. What researchers care about is the wording of the question and the nature of the labels used to anchor the endpoints of the scale (see Dawes & Smith, 1985, for a review), but not the graphic layout in which the scale is presented. Hence, all of the scales shown in Fig. 5.1 are presumably identical, as long as the same verbal endpoint labels are used.

In fact, a perusal of methodology textbooks shows that early discussions of semantic differential scales, for example, most frequently used the graphic presentation format shown in Row d. In later years, this format was replaced by positive and negative numbers, as shown in Row c. More recently, however, the format shown in Row b has become most common. These design decisions reflect shifts in data processing. As long as the answers were counted by hand, the graphical format posed no problem. Once the data were key-punched, presenting numeric values on the questionnaire reduced errors at the data-entry stage. And finally, omitting the minus and plus signs saved the data-typist a keystroke and hence became the dominant format in cost-conscious survey research. Unfortunately, however, these technical decisions are likely to

a.	0	1	2	3	4	5	6
b.	1	2	3	4	5	6	7
c.	-3	-2	-1	0	+1	+2	+3
d.	—-	—	-	-/+	+	+	+++
e.	O	O	O	O	O	O	O

FIG. 5.1. Different formats of rating scales.

influence respondents' interpretation of the meaning of the question, as the following examples demonstrate.

Numeric Values and Scale Polarity

As part of a larger survey, Schwarz, Knäuper, et al.(1991, Experiment 1) asked a quota sample of German adults, "How successful would you say you have been in life?" This question was accompanied by an 11-point rating scale, with the endpoints labeled *not at all successful* and *extremely successful*. To answer this question, respondents have to determine what the researcher means by *not at all successful*. Does this term pertain to the absence of outstanding accomplishments or to the presence of explicit failures? To determine the intended meaning, respondents are likely to draw on any helpful information the researcher may provide. This information includes apparently formal features, such as the numeric values of the rating scale. In the present study, these values ranged either from 0 (*not at all successful*) to 10 (*extremely successful*), or from -5 (*not at all successful*) to +5 (*extremely successful*). The results showed a dramatic impact of the numeric values used, as shown in Table 5.1.

Whereas 34% of the respondents endorsed a value between 0 and 5 on the 0 to 10 scale, only 13% endorsed one of the formally equivalent values between -5 and 0 on the -5 to +5 scale. Coding both scales from 0 to 10, this pattern resulted in mean ratings of $M = 6.4$ on the 0 to 10, but $M = 7.3$ on the -5 to +5 version of the scale. In addition, an inspection of the distributions along both scales indicated that the responses were dislocated toward the high end of the -5 to +5 scale, as compared to the 0 to 10 scale. This is also reflected in markedly different standard deviations, $SDs = 1.03$ and .56 for the 0 to 10 and -5 to +5 scale, respectively.

Subsequent experiments (Schwarz, Knäuper, et al., 1991) indicated that the impact of numeric values is indeed mediated by differential interpretations of the ambiguous endpoint label *not at all successful*. When this label is combined with the numeric value 0, respondents interpret it to refer to the absence of noteworthy success. However, when the same label is combined with the numeric value -5, they interpret it to refer to the presence of explicit failure. This differential interpretation reflects that a minus-to-plus format emphasizes the bipolar nature of the dimension that the

TABLE 5.1
The Impact of Numeric Scale Values on Reports Along Rating Scales

0 to 10 Scale			-5 to +5 Scale		
Scale Value	Percentage	Cumulative	Scale Value	Percentage	Cumulative
0	-	-	-5	1	1
1	-	-	-4	-	1
2	2	2	-3	1	2
3	5	7	-2	1	3
4	7	14	-1	1	4
5	20	34	0	9	13
6	14	48	+1	9	22
7	20	68	+2	23	45
8	20	88	+3	35	80
9	6	94	+4	14	94
10	3	97	+5	4	98
Undecided	3	100	Undecided	2	100
N	480		N	552	

$\chi^2(10) = 105.1, p < .0001$

Note. Percentages rounded. Data based on a quota sample of 1,032 German adults, randomly assigned to conditions (Source: IfD 5007, Juli 1988). Adapted from Schwarz, Knäuper, et al., (1991). Reprinted by permission.

researcher has in mind, implying that one endpoint label refers to the opposite of the other. Hence, *not at all successful* is interpreted as reflecting the opposite of success, that is, failure. In contrast, a rating scale format that presents only positive values suggests that the researcher has a unipolar dimension in mind. In that case, the scale values reflect different degrees of the presence of the crucial feature. Hence, *not at all successful* is now interpreted as reflecting the mere absence of noteworthy success, rather than the presence of failure.

This differential interpretation of the same term as a function of its accompanying numeric value also affects the inferences that judges draw on the basis of a report given along a rating scale. For example, in a follow-up experiment (Schwarz, Knäuper, et al., 1991, Experiment 3), a fictitious student reported his academic success along one of the described scales, checking either a -4 or a formally equivalent 2. As expected, judges who were asked to estimate how often this student had failed an exam assumed that he failed twice as often when he checked a -4 than when he checked a 2, although both values are formally equivalent along the rating scales used.

Similarly, Schwarz and Hippler (1995) asked German respondents to evaluate politicians along an 11-point rating scale, ranging from *don't think very highly of this politician* (0 or -5) to *think very highly of this politician* (11 or +5). Recoding both scales to run from 0 to 10 prior to analysis, they observed that all politicians were rated more positively along the -5 to +5 scale (M = 5.6) than along the 0 to 11 scale (M = 4.9). Again, respondents drew on the numeric values to disambiguate the meaning of the verbal labels. Hence, they interpreted the verbal label *don't think very highly* to indicate the absence of positive thoughts when combined with the numeric value 0, but the presence of negative thoughts when combined with the numeric value -5. Moreover, this effect was as pronounced in telephone interviews, where the scale was presented orally, as in self-administered questionnaires, where the scale was presented visually. Hence, respondents do not need to see the numeric values in a written format to draw on them. Again, the power of these effects becomes particularly apparent when we examine the percentage of respondents who reported values below the respective midpoint of the respective scale. Across both modes of data collection, 29.3% reported a mean approval rating below the midpoint along the -5 to +5 scales, whereas 40.2% did so along the 0 to 10 scales, resulting in a difference of 11.5%. Obviously, politicians interested in a high approval rating fare much better on the former scale.

Beyond Scale Polarity

Moreover, respondents' use of numeric values in making sense of verbal labels is not restricted to variations that include or omit negative numbers. For example, Grayson and Schwarz (1995) asked undergraduates how often they engaged in a variety of low frequency activities. In all conditions, the 11-point rating scale ranged from *rarely* to *often*. However, *rarely* was combined with the numeric value 0 in one condition and the numeric value 1 in the other. As expected, respondents interpreted *rarely* to mean *never* when combined with 0, but to mean *a low frequency* when combined with 1. As a result, they provided higher mean frequency ratings along the 0 to 10 ($M = 2.8$) than the 1 to 11 scale ($M = 1.9$; scale recoded to 0 to 10).

The Graphical Layout of Rating Scales

Much as respondents draw on the numeric values of rating scales in interpreting the meaning of the question, they also extract information about the intended meaning of the question from the scale's graphical layout, as T. Smith (1995) observed. As part of the 1987 International Social Survey Program (ISSP), researchers assessed perceptions of social stratification in nine countries. Specifically, they asked representative samples, "In our society there are groups which tend to be towards the top and groups which tend to be towards the bottom. Below is a scale that runs from top to bottom. Where would you place yourself on this scale?" This question was accompanied by a 10-point rating scale, running from 1 (top) to 10 (bottom). In most affluent nations (e.g., the United States, Germany, or Switzerland), about 10% of the respondents placed themselves at the bottom of the social hierarchy, endorsing a value between 8 and 10. To the researchers' surprise, however, 37.1% of the Dutch respondents did so, in contrast to what one would expect on the basis of the rather homogeneous social stratification of the affluent Netherlands. An inspection of the details of the questionnaires provided an answer to this puzzle.

Specifically, the rating scale was visually displayed as a set of stacked boxes, as shown in Example A of Fig. 5.2, in all countries but the Netherlands. In the Netherlands, the scale was presented in the "shape of a truncated pyramid, with the bottom boxes wider than those in the middle and top" (T. Smith, 1995, p. 4), as shown in Example B. Hence, the Dutch scale may have conveyed that the researcher has a concept of stratification in mind that includes more people at the bottom than in the middle of the social hierarchy. This conceptualization of stratification was not conveyed by the scale used in all other countries, and it is likely that this difference in visual scale display resulted in the surprising deviation in the Dutch data.

Although the interpretation of the Dutch data is ex post, an experimental study provided support for the assumption that respondents draw inferences about the distribution from the graphic layout of the rating scale. Specifically, Schwarz, Grayson, Knäuper, and Wänke (1996) asked U.S. college students to evaluate their academic performance along one of the scales shown in Fig. 5.2. Their question read: "At every university, some students are doing better than others. Some tend to be toward the top of the performance hierarchy and some tend to be toward the bottom. Where would you place your own academic performance?"

The results replicated the differences observed in T. Smith's (1995) analysis of data from different countries. Specifically, students rated their academic performance less favorably ($M = 5.4$) when the pyramid form of the 10-point scale indicated that more students are supposed to be at the bottom of the distribution than when equally sized boxes did not convey this information ($M = 4.0$, $1 =$ top, $10 =$ bottom). In addition, other students were asked to indicate the percentage of students represented by each scale point. Confirming expectations, they assigned more students to the lower scale points when these points were represented by larger boxes.

Conclusions

In combination, the reviewed findings illustrate that apparently minor variations in the format of a rating scale may strongly affect the obtained results, leading us to conclude, for example, that either

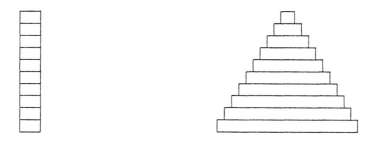

Example A   Example B

Note. Each scale labled $1 =$ top; $10 =$ bottom.

FIG. 5.2.   Visual display of rating scales.

13% or 34% of the population think they were successful in life, that 29% or 40% think highly of a given politician, or that few or many people see themselves at the bottom of the social ladder. Far from indicating meaningless responding, however, these findings suggest that respondents do their best to determine the intended meaning of the question posed to them. Unfortunately, the meaning of the literal question itself is not always clear, reflecting that "even the most unambiguous words show a range of meaning, or a degree of semantic flexibility, ... that is constrained by the particular context in which these words occur" (Woll, Weeks, Fraps, Pendergrass, & Vanderplas, 1980, p. 60). To disambiguate its meaning, respondents turn to the context of the question, much as they would be expected to do in daily life. In a research situation, however, the relevant context includes apparently formal features of questionnaire design, rendering them an important source of information of which respondents make systematic use. This has important methodological implications.

Most obviously, researchers need to be sensitive to the informational implications of their research instrument to guard against unintended interpretations and to use formal features to their advantage. For example, the findings on the numeric values of rating scales suggest that scales that provide a continuum from negative to positive values indicate that the researcher has a bipolar conceptualization of the respective dimension in mind, whereas scales that present only positive values indicate a unipolar conceptualization. If so, the choice of numeric values may either facilitate or dilute the polarity implications of the endpoint labels that are provided to respondents. Researchers may therefore be well advised to match the numeric values that they provide to respondents with the intended conceptualization of the underlying dimension as uni- or bipolar.

Moreover, the reviewed examples highlight the risks associated with an interpretation of the absolute values that respondents report on a rating scale. Depending on the format of the scale, we may arrive at very different conclusions about respondents' opinions, as the ratings of politicians illustrated. Although such absolute interpretations are not very prevalent in psychological research, they are common in the interpretation of opinion polls, despite numerous warnings offered by survey methodologists (see Schuman, 1986).

Finally, the format of the rating scale used may influence our ability to detect relationships with other variables. As illustrated in Table 5.1, for example, rating scales with different numeric values result in differentially skewed distributions. This affects the observed variance and hence the power of subsequent correlational analyses.

FREQUENCY SCALES

That apparently formal features of questionnaires are an important source of information for respondents is further illustrated by research into the impact of response alternatives on behavioral frequency reports and related judgments (see Schwarz, 1990; Schwarz & Hippler, 1987, for reviews). In survey research as well as many psychological studies, respondents are asked to report the frequency with which they engage in a behavior, or experience a certain physical symptom, by checking the appropriate value from a set of frequency response alternatives provided to them. Again, the range of response alternatives may serve as a source of information for respondents. Specifically, respondents assume that the researcher constructed a meaningful scale that reflects his or her knowledge about the distribution of the behavior. Accordingly, values in the middle range of the scale are assumed to reflect the "average" or "typical" behavior, whereas the extremes of the scale are assumed to correspond to the extremes of the distribution. These assumptions influence respondents' interpretation of the question, their behavioral reports, and related judgments.

Question Interpretation

Suppose, for example, that respondents are asked to indicate how frequently they were "really irritated" recently. Before they can give an answer, they must decide what the researcher means by "really irritated." Does this refer to major irritations such as fights with one's spouse or does it refer to minor irritations such as having to wait for service in a restaurant? If the respondents have no opportunity to ask the interviewer for clarification, or if a well-trained interviewer responds, "Whatever you feel is really irritating," they may pick up some pertinent information from the questionnaire. One such piece of information is provided by the frequency range of the response scale.

For example, respondents who are asked to report how often they are irritated on a scale ranging from *several times daily* to *less than once a week* may relate this frequency range to their general knowledge about the frequency of minor and major annoyances. Assuming that major annoyances are unlikely to occur *several times a day*, they may consider instances of less severe irritation to be the target of the question than respondents who are presented a scale ranging from *several times a year* to *less than once every 3 months*. Experimental data support this assumption (Schwarz, Strack, Müller, & Chassein, 1988). Respondents who reported their experiences on the former scale, subsequently reported less extreme examples of annoying experiences than respondents who were given the latter scale. Thus, the type of annoying experiences that respondents reported was determined by the frequency range of the response alternatives in combination with respondents' general knowledge, rather than by the wording of the question per se. Accordingly, the same question combined with different frequency scales is likely to assess different experiences.

Reiterating this point, Gaskell, O'Muircheartaigh, and Wright (1995) observed that the range of frequency response alternatives changed the interpretation of the question, "How often are your teeth cleaned?" When this question was presented with a scale ranging from *less often than once a year* to *more than once a month*, respondents assumed that it referred to getting one's teeth cleaned by a dental hygienist. But when presented with a scale ranging from *more than once a day* to *less often than once a week*, they assumed that the question pertained to their own brushing or flossing.

Theoretically, the impact of the response alternatives on respondents' interpretation of the question should be more pronounced the less clearly the target behavior is defined. For this reason, questions about subjective experiences may be particularly sensitive to the impact of response alternatives because researchers usually refrain from providing a detailed definition of the target experience so as not to interfere with its subjective nature. Ironically, assessing the frequency of a behavior with precoded response alternatives may result in doing just what is avoided in the wording of the question.

Frequency Estimates

Even if the behavior under investigation is well defined, however, the range of response alternatives may strongly affect respondents' frequency estimates. As many studies demonstrated, mundane behaviors of a high frequency, such as watching television, for example, are not represented in memory as distinct episodes (see Bradburn, Rips, & Shevell, 1987; Schwarz, 1990, for reviews). Rather, the various episodes blend together in a generic representation of the behavior that lacks temporal markers. When asked how often they engage in such a behavior, respondents can therefore not recall the episodes to determine the frequency of the behavior. Instead, they have to rely on estimation strategies to arrive at an answer (see Sudman, Bradburn, & Schwarz, 1996, chapters 7 and 9, for a more detailed discussion). In doing so, they may use the range of the scale presented to them as a frame of reference. This results in higher frequency estimates along scales that present high rather than low frequency response alternatives.

The results of a study on television consumption, shown in Table 5.2, illustrate this effect (Schwarz et al., 1985, Experiment 1). In this study, 37.5% of a quota sample of German adults reported watching television for 2.5 hours or more a day, when presented with the high frequency response alternatives shown in Table 5.2, whereas only 16.2% reported doing so when presented with the low frequency response alternatives. Subsequent studies replicated this frequency estimation effect for a wide range of behaviors, including

TABLE 5.2
**Reported Daily TV Consumption as a Function
of Response Alternatives**

Low Frequency Alternatives		High Frequency Alternatives	
Up to 1/2 hour	7.4%	Up to 2.5 hours	62.5%
1/2 hour to 1 hour	17.7%	2.5 hours to 3 hours	23.4%
1 hour to 1.5 hours	26.5%	3 hours to 3.5 hours	7.8%
1.5 hours to 2 hours	14.7%	3.5 hours to 4 hours	4.7%
2 hours to 2.5 hours	17.7%	4 hours to 4.5 hours	1.6%
More than 2.5 hours	16.2%	More than 4.5 hours	0.0%

Note. $N = 132$. Adapted from Schwarz, et al. (1985). Reprinted by permission.

the frequency of doctor visits, headaches, alcohol consumption, masturbation, and consumer behaviors (e.g., Billiet, Loosveldt, & Waterplas, 1988; Gaskell, O'Muircheartaigh, & Wright, 1994; Menon, Rhagubir, & Schwarz, 1995; Schwarz, 1990; Schwarz & Bienias, 1990; Schwarz & Scheuring, 1988, 1991).

Not surprisingly, respondents' reliance on the frame of reference suggested by the response alternatives increases as their knowledge about relevant episodes decreases (Menon et al., 1995; Schwarz & Bienias, 1990), or the complexity of the judgmental task increases (Bless, Bohner, Hild, & Schwarz, 1992). More importantly, however, the impact of response alternatives is completely eliminated when the informational value of the response alternatives is called into question. For example, telling respondents that they are participating in a pretest designed to explore the adequacy of the response alternatives, or informing student subjects that the scale was taken from a survey of the elderly, wiped out the otherwise obtained impact of response alternatives (Schwarz & Hippler, 1990). Again, these findings illustrate that respondents assume the researcher to be a cooperative communicator, whose contributions are relevant to the ongoing conversation, unless the implicit guarantee of relevance is called into question.

Comparative Judgments

In addition, the frequency range of the response alternatives has been found to affect subsequent comparative judgments. Given the assumption that the scale reflects the distribution of the behavior, checking a response alternative is the same as locating one's own position in the distribution. Accordingly, respondents extract comparison information from their own location on the response scale and use this information in making subsequent comparative judgments.

For example, checking 2 hours on the low frequency scale shown in Table 5.2 implies that a respondent's television consumption is above average, whereas checking the same value on the high frequency scale implies that his or her television consumption is below average. As a result, respondents in the Schwarz et al. (1985) studies reported that television plays a more important role in their leisure time (Experiment 1) when they had to report their television consumption on the low rather than high frequency scale, although the same respondents had just reported watching less television in the first place. Moreover, other respondents described themselves as less satisfied with the variety of things they do in their leisuretime when the low frequency response scale suggested that they watch more television than most other people (Experiment 2).

Again, the impact of scale range on comparative judgments has been replicated across a wide range of behaviors and judgments. For example, Schwarz and Scheuring (1988) observed that respondents reported lower satisfaction with their intimate relationship, and higher interest in extramarital affairs, when the range of response alternatives suggested that their masturbation frequency is above, rather than below, average. Similarly, patients of a psychosomatic clinic reported higher satisfaction with their health when they had to report the frequency of psychosomatic symptoms along a scale with high rather than low response alternatives, again reflecting that the high frequency scale suggested that their symptom frequency is below average. Moreover, this effect was obtained despite the fact that the high frequency scale resulted in higher reports of symptom frequency in the first place (Schwarz & Scheuring, 1992).

Finally, these frame-of-reference effects are not limited to respondents themselves, but influence the users of their reports as well, as a study on medical decision making may illustrate (Schwarz, Bless, et al., 1991, Experiment 2). Specifically, we asked first-year students of medicine and practicing medical doctors (with an average professional experience of 8.5 years) to participate in a study designed to "test if a standard health survey could be shortened without a decrease in usefulness and reliability." As part of this study, subjects had to evaluate the severity of several symptom reports that were presented to them in the context of the high or low frequency scales shown in Fig. 5.3.

For example, in one vignette, "Mr. Z., 25 years old" checked that he suffered twice a week from "aching loins or back," and in another vignette, "Mrs. K., 41 years old" checked that she suffered from a "lack of energy," also twice a week. Note that "twice a week" constitutes a high response on the low frequency scale, but a low response on the high frequency scale. Doctors were asked to rate the severity of the reported symptom (0 = *not at all severe* to 10 = *very severe*) and the necessity to consult a doctor (0 = *not at all necessary to consult a doctor* to 10 = *absolutely necessary to consult a doctor*). Table 5.3 shows the results.

Low Frequency Scale

()	()	()	()	()	()
less than once a month	about once a month	about once in 2 weeks	about once a week	about twice a week	more often

High Frequency Scale

()	()	()	()	()	()
less than twice a week	about twice a week	about four times a week	about six times a week	about once every 24 hours	more often

FIG. 5.3.   Response scales for medical symptom reports.

TABLE 5.3
**Mean Severity and Consultation Necessity Ratings
as a Function of Scale Range and Expertise**

	Expertise			
	Doctors		Students	
	Frequency Range of Scale			
	High	Low	High	Low
Severity of Symptoms				
Aching loins or back	3.09	4.72	4.94	5.95
Lack of energy	2.30	4.13	2.92	5.35
Necessity to Consult Doctor				
Aching loins or back	4.48	6.25	6.00	7.07
Lack of energy	3.42	4.62	3.06	5.15

Note. Range of values is 0 to 10; higher values indicate higher severity and higher necessity to consult a doctor. Adapted from Schwarz, Bless, et al. (1991). Reprinted by permission.

As expected, suffering from a given symptom "twice a week" was rated as more severe, and as more likely to require consultation, when "twice a week" represented a high rather than a low frequency response on the respective scale. Moreover, the impact of scale range was independent of subjects' expertise, and was obtained for experienced practitioners as well as first-year students. In fact, the only expertise effect that emerged reflected that first-year medical students were more likely to consider all symptoms as severe and to recommend consultation under most conditions.

Conclusions

Again, the reviewed findings illustrate how apparently irrelevant variations in question format may strongly affect the obtained results, introducing systematic bias. After all, reports of television consumption or symptom frequency should be based on recollections of one's actual behavior, rather than on the scale presented by the researcher. Given that frequent episodes of the same behavior blend into a generic representation that lacks time and space markers (see Bradburn et al., 1987; Schwarz, 1990; Sudman et al., 1996, for reviews), however, respondents are unable to recall relevant episodes and count their number, in contrast to what the researcher would want them to do. Hence, they try to come up with a reasonable estimate and they rely on information that seems highly relevant to their task, namely the response scale provided by the researcher. Assuming that the researcher is an expert on the issue under investigation, respondents believe that the scale reflects expert knowledge about the distribution of the behavior. When this assumption is called into question, the impact of scale range is attenuated. Unless informed otherwise, however, respondents have little reason to assume that the researcher constructed a haphazard scale and are therefore extracting relevant information that serves as input into frequency estimates and comparative judgments.

Although we may be willing to tolerate that laypeople rely on the information provided by a response scale when they respond to a survey question, we may find it less tolerable that our doctors may do so when rendering professional judgments. However, the only information that was available to the physicians in the study mentioned here was the patient's checkmark on a frequency scale, pertaining to one single symptom. In contrast, physicians usually attend to constellations of multiple symptoms in clinical practice. But in the absence of more useful covariation information, the only thing they could draw on was the relative placement of the reported symptom frequency in the distribution of symptom frequencies suggested by the scale. And like respondents in surveys, they had little reason to doubt the relevance of the scale presented to them, given that it was presented as part of a "standard health survey," which was presumably developed by people who knew what they were doing.

Finally, the methodological implications of the reviewed findings deserve some attention (see Schwarz, 1990; Schwarz & Hippler, 1987, for more detailed discussions). First, the numeric response alternatives presented as part of a frequency question may influence respondents' interpretation of what the question refers to. Hence, the same question stem in combination with different frequency alternatives may result in the assessment of somewhat different behaviors. This is more likely the less well defined the behavior is. Second, respondents' use of the response scale as a frame of reference influences the obtained behavioral reports. Aside from calling the interpretation of the absolute values into question, this also implies that reports of the same behavior along different scales are not comparable, often rendering comparisons between different studies difficult.

Third, even when we are not interested in respondents' absolute behavioral frequencies, the impact of response scales may undermine comparisons between groups of respondents as well as comparisons across behaviors. Suppose, for example, that some respondents' behavioral frequencies are well represented by the scale, whereas others are not. Relying on the scale as a frame of reference, both groups of respondents are nevertheless likely to arrive at similar estimates. As a result, the obtained reports would underestimate real differences in the sample. Similarly, reports of behaviors that are poorly represented in memory are more likely to be affected than reports of behaviors that are well represented. Hence, the stronger impact of scale range on the more poorly represented behavior may either exaggerate or reduce differences in the reported frequency of both behaviors. As these possibilities illustrate, the range of frequency scales may not only affect our inferences about respondents' absolute behavioral frequencies, but also our inferences about differences between specific groups or specific behaviors. Finally, respondents' use of the comparison information conveyed by the scale may influence subsequent comparative judgments, even under conditions where respondents' own behavior is sufficiently well represented in memory to be immune to response scale effects (e.g., Menon et al., 1995).

To avoid these biases, researchers are well advised to ask behavioral frequency questions in an open response format. In doing so, however, it is important to structure the question in a way that elicits numeric responses rather than vague verbal answers. Despite the widespread use of the format illustrated in Table 5.2, a simpler question would do a better job: "How many hours a day do you watch television? __ hours a day."

THE IMPACT OF OPEN VERSUS CLOSED QUESTION FORMATS

The examples reviewed so far indicate that respondents draw on formal features of a questionnaire in interpreting ambiguous questions, using, for example, the numeric values of rating scales to determine the meaning of verbal scale labels. Understanding the literal meaning of a question, however, is not enough to answer it, as is seen in more detail in the next chapter. Rather, respondents also have to determine the pragmatic meaning of a question, that is which information the questioner is interested in and hence wants them to provide. Suppose, for example, that you are asked to report what you have done today. Most likely, you would not include in your report that you took a shower, got dressed, and so on. If these activities were included in a list of response alternatives, however, you would probably endorse them. This thought experiment reflects a set of standard findings from the survey methodology literature (see Schwarz & Hippler, 1991, for a review).

Experimental studies on the impact of open- and closed-response formats have consistently demonstrated that these formats yield considerable differences in the marginal distribution as well as the ranking of items (e.g., Bishop, Hippler, Schwarz, & Strack, 1988; Schuman & Presser, 1977). On the one hand, any given opinion is less likely to be volunteered in an open-response format than to be endorsed in a closed-response format, if presented. On the other hand, opinions that are omitted from the set of response alternatives in a closed format are unlikely to be reported at all, even if an "other" category is explicitly offered, which respondents in general rarely use (Bradburn, 1983; Molenaar, 1982). Several processes are likely to contribute to these findings.

Most importantly, respondents are unlikely to spontaneously report, in an open-answer format, information that seems self-evident or irrelevant. In refraining from these responses they follow the conversational maxim that an utterance should be informative and should provide the information that the recipient is interested in. This results in an underreporting of presumably self-evident information that is eliminated by closed-response formats, where the explicit presentation of the proper response alternative indicates the investigator's interest in this information. Moreover, respondents may frequently be uncertain if information that comes to mind does or does not belong to the domain of information the investigator is interested in. Again, closed-response formats may reduce this uncertainly, resulting in higher responses. Finally, a generic "other" response provides little information and would be considered inadequate as an answer in most conversations. Hence, it is rarely checked.

In addition, the response alternatives may remind respondents of options that they may otherwise not have considered. The literature in survey methodology has typically focused on this latter possibility, implying that closed response formats may suggest answers that respondents would never think of themselves. This assumption is to some degree supported by the observation that less educated respondents are more likely to refuse to answer in an open-response format, but to provide an answer in a closed-response format, than well-educated respondents (Schuman & Presser, 1981). However, a conversational analysis suggests that the obtained differences are more plausibly traced to the clarification of the questioner's interest that is provided by a closed-response format. Most importantly, the assumption that respondents may lack the information required for an answer, and hence pick one from the response alternatives, may hold to some degree for complex knowledge questions, but does not hold for questions about daily activities, such as, "What have you done today?" Nevertheless, the same differences are obtained for questions of this type, and they are most pronounced for activities that the questioner may take for granted anyway, such as taking a shower or having breakfast (see Schwarz, Hippler, & Noelle-Neumann, 1994, for a more extended discussion).

HAVING OR NOT HAVING AN OPINION: "DON'T KNOW" OPTIONS AND FILTER QUESTIONS

As noted in the discussion of fictitious issues (chapter 4), public opinion researchers are often concerned that survey respondents may make up an opinion when asked, even though they may never have thought about the issue before the question was asked. To avoid such "doorstep" opinions, survey researchers frequently use "no opinion" filters to screen out respondents who may not hold an opinion on the issue under investigation. This is either accomplished by offering a "no opinion" option as part of a set of precoded response alternatives (often referred to as a *quasi-filter*), or by asking respondents if they have an opinion on the issue before the question proper is asked (often referred to as a *full filter*).

Research on the use of filter questions (see Bishop, Oldendick, & Tuchfarber, 1983; Schuman & Presser, 1981; Schwarz & Hippler, 1991, for reviews) indicates that respondents are more likely to endorse a "no opinion" option if it is explicitly offered than to volunteer it. Moreover, they are more likely to report not having an opinion on the issue if a full filter is used than if a "no opinion" option is offered as part of the response alternatives—and the more so, the more strongly the full filter is worded. For example, asking respondents if they have an opinion on the issue results in fewer "no opinion" responses than asking them if they "have thought enough about the issue to have an opinion on it" (Bishop et al., 1983). Survey researchers often assume that respondents find it embarrassing to admit that they do not have an opinion on an issue and hence "make up" an answer. Providing them with a "don't know" option presumably reduces the pressure to provide an answer, and the more so, the more explicitly this possibility is introduced.

It is informative, however, to ask what respondents learn about the nature of their task when we ask them, "Have you thought enough about this issue to have an opinion on it?" Most likely, they will infer that we are not interested in their gut response or in any global preferences they may have. Rather, we are presumably asking for a careful assessment of the issue, based on considerable knowledge of the facts. If so, respondents may also assume that we will ask them many detailed questions that will require considerable knowledge. Experimental data confirmed these conjectures.

Hippler and Schwarz (1989, Experiments 1 and 2) presented German respondents with the statement, "The Russians are basically trying to get along with America," and asked them one of the following questions:

1. Do you agree or disagree, or do you have no opinion on this?
   ( ) agree
   ( ) disagree
   ( ) have no opinion
2. Do you have an opinion on this?
   ( ) no, have no opinion
   ( ) yes, have opinion"
3. Have you thought enough about this issue to have an opinion on it?
   ( ) no, have no opinion
   ( ) yes, have opinion

After having provided an answer, respondents were asked to report their expectations about subsequent questions they may be asked. As predicted, respondents who received Question 3 expected more, and more difficult, follow-up questions, and assumed that they would be less likely to have the required knowledge to answer them, than respondents who received Question 1. The expectations of respondents who received Question 2 fell in between these extremes.

These and related findings (see Hippler & Schwarz, 1989; Trometer, 1994) suggest that the use of filter questions may discourage respondents from giving substantive answers: The stronger the filter, the more respondents assume that they are facing a difficult task—and the less likely they are to provide a substantive response, as many previous studies have shown. Accordingly, the use of filter questions may result in an underestimation of the number of respondents who hold an opinion at the level of specificity that the question requires: Respondents who may well hold an opinion may be unlikely to report doing so because they expect a more demanding task than they actually would have to face.

CONCLUSIONS

Findings of the type reviewed here are usually considered measurement "artifacts." From a conversational point of view, however, they simply reflect that respondents bring the assumptions that govern the conduct of conversations in daily life to the research situation. Hence, they assume that every contribution is relevant to the goal of the ongoing conversation—and in a research situation, these contributions include apparently formal features of the questionnaire, such as the numeric values presented as part of a rating scale or the response alternatives presented as part of a frequency question. As a result, the scales used are far from being "neutral" measurement devices. Rather, they constitute a source of information that respondents actively use in determining their task and in constructing a reasonable answer. Although research methodologists have traditionally focused on the information that is provided by the wording of the question, we need to pay equal attention to the information that is conveyed by apparently formal features of the questionnaire.

6

Making One's Contribution Informative: The Changing Meaning of Redundant Questions

The research reviewed in the preceding chapters illustrated how many apparent biases and shortcomings in human judgment or artifacts in opinion measurement may, in part, be traced to the implicit guarantee of relevance that characterizes human communication. However, the maxims of cooperative communication do not only determine recipients' use of the information provided by speakers. Rather, they also determine what information the recipient of a question is expected to provide in turn. Specifically, cooperative speakers are supposed to provide information that is relevant to the goal of the conversation. This not only implies that the provided information should be substantively related to the topic of the conversation. Rather, it also implies that the provided information should be new to the recipient (Clark & Clark, 1977). Hence, the utterance should not reiterate information that the recipient already has, or may take for granted anyway, as such repetitons would violate the maxim of quantity. Accordingly, determining which information one should provide requires extensive inferences about the information that the recipient has, to identify what is, or is not, "informative." As was the case for information (inadvertently) provided by the researcher, conversational rules that govern the selection of information to be provided by research participants underlie many apparently surprising findings in social and psychological research.

REPEATED QUESTIONS AND CHANGING ANSWERS

In this section, I focus on two phenomena that have rarely been considered as related, namely children's performance on Piagetian conservation tasks and the emergence of context effects in attitude judgments. Both of these phenomena reflect, in part, that the repetition of highly similar questions results in differential interpretations of question meaning and hence in different answers: Unless the person asked has reason to believe that the questioner did not understand the answer given in response to the first question, he or she is likely to interpret the second question as a request for *new* information. Hence, the answer given to the second question will differ from the previously provided answer in predictable ways. The studies reviewed here illustrate these shifting interpretations and their impact on respondents' reports—as well as the misleading conclusions that have been drawn from them.

Experimenters' Questions and Children's Cognitive Skills: The Piagetian Conservation Task

Much as researchers' violations of conversational norms have contributed to overestimations of adults' cognitive biases, they have also contributed to underestimations of children's cognitive skills. Research on the conservation task introduced by Piaget (1952; Piaget & Inhelder, 1969) may serve as an example. In a typical study, a child is shown two rows of objects, equal in number and aligned in one-to-one correspondence, as shown in the first column of Fig. 6.1. When asked, "Is there more here or more here, or are both the same number?", the child usually answers that both rows are the same in number. Next, the experimenter rearranges the objects in one of the rows to extend the row's length, as shown in the second column of Fig. 6.1. Following this transformation, the previously asked question is repeated, "Is there more here or more here, or are both the same number?" Many young children now respond that there are more objects in the longer row, suggesting that they did not master number conservation.

Given that only the perceptual configuration of the crucial row has changed, explanations of this phenomenon have typically focused on children's susceptibility to perceptual influences. How-

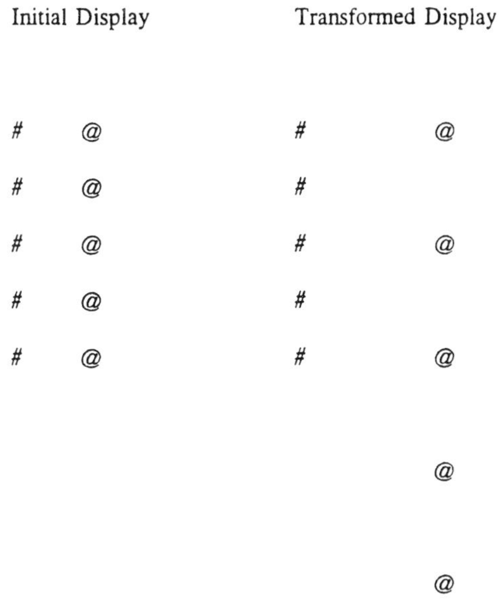

	Initial Display		Transformed Display
#	@	#	@
#	@	#	
#	@	#	@
#	@	#	
#	@	#	@
			@
			@

FIG. 6.1. Number conservation

ever, a conversational analysis of the procedures used proves informative. Why would a speaker ask the same question twice within a very short time span, unless he or she inquired about some new aspect? And what would that new aspect most likely be, following the deliberate and intentional transformation performed by the questioner? As McGarrigle and Donaldson (1974) noted, in early stages of language acquisition, children use the behavior of a speaker "to arrive at a notion of speaker's meaning and this knowledge is utilized to make sense of the language around"(p. 347) them, much as adults use the context of an utterance to disambiguate its meaning. From this perspective, "it could be that the experimenter's simple direct action of changing the length of the row leads the child to infer an intention on the experimenter's part to talk about what he has just been doing. It is as if the experimenter refers behaviorally to length although he continues to talk about number" (p. 343).[1]

---

[1]Thanks to Denis Hilton for making me aware of this line of research.

To test this assumption, McGarrigle and Donaldson conducted a study in which they varied the apparent intentionality of the transformation. Whereas they replicated the standard procedure in one condition, a "naughty teddy bear" appeared in the other and tried to "spoil the game" by rearranging the objects, increasing the length of one row. The results provided strong support for a conversational account: Whereas only 13 out of 80 children showed number conservation when the experimenter manipulated the length of the row, 50 out of the same 80 children showed number conservation when the change was due to the apparently unintended interference of "naughty teddy." These findings suggest that the children used the behavioral context of the question to infer the speaker's meaning: When "naughty teddy" changed the arrangement of the objects, the experimenter may indeed want to know if teddy took an object or if the number remained the same. But repeating the previously answered number question makes little sense when the experimenter changed the arrangement himself, leading children to infer that the experimenter apparently wants to talk about what he did, thus changing the reference of the question from number to length.

Subsequent studies by Dockrell, Neilson, and Campbell (1980); Light, Buckingham, and Robbins (1979); and Hargreaves, Molloy, and Pratt (1982) confirmed this conclusion (see Donaldson, 1982, for a review). For example, Light and colleagues studied the conservation of quantity using glass beakers that contained small pasta shells. Because the pasta shells were to be used in a competitive game, it was important that both players had equal amounts of shells. After the children confirmed that there was the same amount of shells in both beakers, the experimenter transferred the shells from one beaker into another one of a different shape, thus changing the appearance. In one condition, this was done without an apparent reason and the standard question was repeated. In another condition, however, the experimenter suddenly noticed that one of the beakers had a badly chipped rim, making it unsafe to use. Looking around the room, he picked a beaker of a different shape and transferred the shells. The difference between both conditions was dramatic: Whereas only 5% of the children in the standard condition showed number conservation, confirming that both beakers contain the same amount of shells, 70% of the children in the "chipped rim" condition did so. Again, the findings suggest that reiterating the same question without a plausible reason for doing so results in shifts in question interpretation, which are not obtained when the reiteration is legitimized by the context in which it occurs.

That the changes in children's interpretation of the question are indeed driven by conversationally inappropriate question reiteration has been nicely demonstrated by Rose and Blank (1974). In their study, children were again shown two rows of equal length with the same number of objects, but only some of the children had to make an initial judgment at this point. Subsequently, the experimenter changed the arrangement, increasing the length of one row. As usual, many of the children who had already given a judgment when the rows were equal now reported that the longer row has more objects. However, children who had not previously been asked were considerably more likely to respond that the number of objects in both rows is the same (see also Siegal, Waters, & Dinwiddy, 1988). Clearly, it is not children's confusion of number and length per se that leads them astray. Rather, having already answered the question, the children assume that the experimenter must have something else in mind when the question is reiterated. Hence, they respond to their new interpretation of the reiterated question, unless asking for the same information twice makes sense, as was the case in McGarrigle and Donaldson's (1974) study and related experiments.

This interpretation of "incorrect" conservation responses obviously raises the question why older children perform better than younger children under standard conditions? What is it that develops with increasing age? I surmise that the answer lies, in part, in children's increasing experience that adults may ask questions to which the questioner obviously knows the answer. The most prominent example of these questions are "exam" questions designed to assess the answerer's knowledge rather than to acquire needed information about the topic. When children understand this special form of questioning, and interpret the experimental situation as one of its instantiations, question repetition should be less likely to lead them astray (cf. Elbers, 1986).

Finally, it is worth noting that meaning shifts as a result of question repetition may also underlie other findings in the developmental literature, such as Kohlberg and Ullian's (1974) observation that young children may not recognize that a person's gender remains constant irrespective of clothing or toy preferences. As in the conservation experiments reviewed here, the relevant experimental procedure involves repeated questions about a target's gender after features of the target's appearance are changed (e.g., Slaby & Frey, 1975; Smetana & Letourneau, 1984). Again, it is conceivable that children assume that the experimenter knows as well as they do that gender doesn't change, and hence must refer to appearance rather than gender when the same question is reiterated.

Repeating Similar Questions in Attitude Surveys: Are "Happiness" and "Satisfaction" the Same Thing?

Much as children have been found to change their interpretation of the same question if reiterated within a short time span, adults have been observed to change, or not to change, their interpretation of highly similar questions as a function of the conversational context in which the questions are posed. For example, Strack et al. (1991, Experiment 2) asked German students to rate their happiness and satisfaction with life as a whole along 11-point scales (11 = *very happy* or *very satisfied*, respectively). In one condition, both questions were presented at the end of the same questionnaire and were introduced by a joint lead-in that read, "Now, we have two questions about your life." In the other condition, only the happiness question was presented at the end of the questionnaire, introduced by a parallel lead-in, "Now, we have a question about your life." The subsequent rating of life satisfaction, however, was presented as the first question in a new and ostensibly unrelated questionnaire about characteristics of research participants, attributed to a different researcher and presented in a different graphic layout.

How would these manipulations affect respondents' interpretation of the concepts *happiness* and *satisfaction*? In general, happiness and satisfaction are perceived as closely related concepts and both judgments have typically been found to be affected by the same variables in studies of subjective well-being (see Schwarz, 1987; Schwarz & Strack, 1991). However, when both questions are presented as part of the same conversational context, interpreting them as nearly identical in meaning would result in considerable redundancy. Hence, respondents may infer that the researcher intends both questions to tap different aspects of their subjective well-being and may, accordingly, draw on different information about their life in making their judgments. Note, however, that this does not apply when the questions are asked by two different communicators. In this case, both communicators may simply use somewhat different words to refer to the same thing and providing identical responses would not violate the norm of nonredundancy, given that each response is directed to a different recipient. As a result, the answers given to both questions should be more similar when the questions are asked by different researchers rather than by the same researcher.

Strack et al.'s (1991, Experiment 2) findings confirmed this expectation. When both questions were asked in ostensibly unrelated questionnaires, subjects' mean reports of happiness ($M = 8.0$) and satisfaction ($M = 8.2$) did not differ and both measures correlated $r = .96$. When both questions were presented as part of the same conversational context, however, subjects reported significantly higher happiness ($M = 8.1$) than satisfaction ($M = 7.4$) and the correlation between both measures dropped significantly to $r = .75$. Apparently, respondents inferred from the conversational relatedness of both questions that the researcher must have distinct concepts in mind, as asking the same thing twice would make little sense. Accordingly, they presumably based their responses on different aspects of their life under this condition, a process that is shown more clearly in the studies reviewed next.

ANSWERING QUESTIONS OF A DIFFERENT GENERALITY: THE EMERGENCE OF ASSIMILATION AND CONTRAST EFFECTS

Although reiterating the same question renders the question as a whole redundant, other questions may only be partially redundant. This is the case when two related questions of different generality are posed. For example, respondents may be asked how satisfied they are with their marriage, as well as how satisfied they are with their life as a whole. In this case, the two questions stand in a part–whole relationship to one another, with the specific question pertaining to a subset of the content domain addressed in the general question. Question sequences of this type have been found to result in pronounced context effects in attitude measurement (see Schuman & Presser, 1981; Turner & Martin, 1984, for examples). However, the exact nature of these context effects has often been difficult to predict and contrast as well as assimilation effects have been observed. In this section, I first summarize the key assumptions of a general model of the emergence of context effects in attitude measurement and subsequently explore the interplay of cognitive and conversational processes in the emergence of assimilation and contrast effects.

The Inclusion—Exclusion Model of Assmilation and Contrast Effects

Forming an attitude judgment requires a mental representation of the to-be-evaluated target as well as a mental representation of some standard. Schwarz and Bless (1992a) proposed that both representations are constructed on the spot and include chronically as well as temporarily accessible information. Whereas the chronically accessible information results in some stability in the obtained judgments, temporarily accessible information provides the basis for context effects in attitude measurement. Information that is included in the representation of the target results in *assimilation effects*. That is, including information with positive implications results in a more positive judgment, whereas including information with negative implications results in a more negative judgment. The size of assimilation effects increases with the amount and extremity of temporarily accessible information and decreases with the amount and extremity of chronically accessible information included in the representation of the target. These set size effects reflect that the judgment is based on the implications of the information included in the representation formed of the target.

Contrast effects, on the other hand, reflect the exclusion of information from the representation of the target. Contrast effects may take two different forms. First, some positive (or negative) piece of information may be excluded from the representation of the target, resulting in a representation that includes less positive (or negative) information. As a result, the judgment formed on the basis of this representation is less positive (or negative), reflecting a contrast effect. The size of such *subtraction*-based contrast effects increases with the amount and extremity of the excluded information and decreases with the amount and extremity of the information that remains in the representation of the target. As a second possibility, the excluded information may be used in constructing a standard of comparison, resulting in a more positive (or negative) standard against which the target is compared. The size of such *comparison*-based contrast effects increases with the amount and extremity of the information included in the representation formed of the standard and decreases with the amount and extremity of chronically accessible information included in the standard. Whereas subtraction-based contrast effects are limited to the evaluation of the target from which the information is excluded, comparison-based contrast effects generalize to all targets to which the standard is applicable (see Schwarz & Bless, 1992a, for examples and a more detailed discussion).

The model assumes that the default operation is to include information that comes to mind in the representation of the target, whereas the exclusion of information needs to be triggered by task characteristics or situational influences. These triggering conditions can be conceptualized in terms of three broad decisions bearing on the use of information that comes to mind. The first decision pertains to whether the information that comes to mind "belongs" to the target category or not. Variables such as the width of the target category (e.g., Schwarz & Bless, 1992b) or the representativeness of the information for the target category (e.g., Strack, Schwarz, & Gschneidinger, 1985) determine inclusion or exclusion at this stage. A second decision bears on why the information comes to mind. If respondents are aware that some information may only come to mind because it has been primed by a preceding task, for example, they may correct for undue influences by excluding the information from the representation of the target (e.g., Lombardi, Higgins, & Bargh, 1987; Strack, Schwarz, Bless, Kübler, & Wänke, 1993). Finally, respondents may exclude information that comes to mind because its repeated use would violate the conversational norm of nonredundancy. This may be the case when they have already answered a specific question (e.g., pertaining to their marital happiness) and are subsequently asked a more general one (e.g., pertaining to their general life satisfaction). In this case, they may include the information brought to mind by the specific question in the representation formed to answer the general question if the two questions are perceived as unrelated. This inclusion would result in an assimilation effect. If the two questions are seen as part of the same conversational context, however, respondents may try to avoid redundancy by deliberately excluding information that they have already provided in response to the specific question when they are later asked the general one. This would result in a contrast effect. These possibilities have been entertained by different researchers (e.g., Bradburn, 1982; Strack & Martin, 1987; Tourangeau, 1984) and the studies reviewed next bear on this conversational determinant of the emergence of assimilation and contrast effects. I first address differences in the emerging correlations and subsequently turn to the somewhat more complex issue of differences in the means.

General and Specific Judgments: Differences in Correlation

To explore the relationship between related judgments of differential generality, Schwarz, Strack, and Mai (1991) asked respondents to report how satisfied they are with their marriage or intimate relationship as well as with their life as a whole, varying the order in which both questions were asked in a self-administered questionnaire. The first column of Table 6.1 shows the resulting correlations between marital and life satisfaction. When the life satisfaction question preceded the marital satisfaction question, both measures were moderately correlated, $r = .32$. In a second condition, however, the question order was reversed and the marital satisfaction question was presented as the last question on one page and the life satisfaction question as the first question on the next

TABLE 6.1
Correlation of Relationship Satisfaction and Life-Satisfaction as a Function of Question Order and Conversational Context

Condition	Number of Specific Questions	
	One	Three
General–specific	.32*	.32*
Specific–general	.67*	.46*
Specific–general, with joint lead-in	.18	.48*
Specific–general, explicit inclusion	.61*	.53*
Specific–general, explicit exclusion	.20	.11

Note. $N = 50$ per cell, except for "Specific–general with joint lead-in," $N = 56$. Correlations marked by an asterisk differ from chance, $p < .05$. Adapted from Schwarz, Strack, and Mai (1991). Reprinted by permission.

page of the same questionnaire. In this case the correlation increased to $r = .67$. This reflects that answering the marital satisfaction question increased the accessibility of marriage related information in memory. As a result, respondents were more likely to include marriage related information in the representation that they formed of their life as a whole, resulting in an assimilation effect (see Schwarz & Strack, 1991, for a more general discussion of judgments of subjective well-being). This interpretation is supported by a highly similar correlation of $r = .61$ in a control condition where the general question explicitly asked respondents to include their marriage in evaluating their overall life satisfaction.

In another condition, however, Schwarz et al. deliberately evoked the conversational norm of nonredundancy. To do so, both questions were placed on the same page of the questionnaire and were introduced by a joint lead-in, "We now have two questions about your life. The first pertains to your marital satisfaction and the second to your general life-satisfaction." Under this condition, the same question order that resulted in $r = .67$ without a joint lead-in, now produced a low and nonsignificant correlation or $r = .18$. This suggests that respondents deliberately excluded information that they had already provided in response to the marital satisfaction question when they were subsequently asked to evaluate their general life satisfaction. Apparently, they interpreted the general question as if it referred to aspects of their life that they had not yet reported on. In line with this interpretation, a control condition in which respondents were explicitly asked how satisfied they are with "other aspects" of their life, "aside from their relationship," yielded a nearly identical correlation of $r = .20$.

In a subsequent study, Schwarz and Hippler (1992) observed that the conversational norm of nonredundancy may not only be evoked by a joint lead-in, but also by the graphic layout of a questionnaire. Specifically, the marital satisfaction question and the general question were either presented in separate boxes, with a black frame drawn around each question, or in a joint box, with one frame drawn around both questions. As in the data just presented, increasing the conversational relatedness of both questions by presenting them in one box significantly reduced the otherwise obtained correlation, again illustrating the conversational relevance of apparently formal features of questionnaires (see chapter 5).

Note, however, that the applicability of the norm of nonredundancy may vary as a function of the number of specific questions that precede the more general one. If only one specific question precedes the general one, the repeated use of the information on which the answer to the specific question was based results in redundancy in the response to the general question. Hence, this repeated use of the same information is avoided if both questions are assigned to the same conversational context, as the data here demonstrated. Suppose, however, that several specific questions precede the general one. For example, respondents may be asked to report on their marital satisfaction, their job satisfaction, and their leisuretime satisfaction before a general life satisfaction question is presented. In this case, they may interpret the general question in two different ways. On the one hand, they may assume that it is a request to consider still other aspects of their life, much as if it were worded, "In addition to what you already told us. . ." On the other hand, they may interpret the general question as a request to integrate the previously reported aspects into an overall judgment, much as if it were worded, "Taking these aspects together, how satisfied are you with your life as a whole?" Note that this interpretational ambiguity of the general question does not arise if only one specific question was asked. In this case, an interpretation of the general question in the sense of "taking all aspects together" would make little sense because only one aspect was addressed, thus rendering this interpretation of the general question completely redundant with the specific one. If several specific questions were asked, however, both interpretations of the general question are viable. In this case, the interpretation of the general question as a request for a final integrative summary judgment is legitimate from a conversational point of view. If several specific questions have been asked, an integrative judgment is informative because it does provide "new" information about the relative importance of the respective domains, which are in the focus of the conversation. Moreover, "summing up" at the end of a series of related thoughts is acceptable conversational practice—whereas there is little to sum up if only one thought was offered. Accordingly, respondents may interpret a general question as a request for a summary judgment if it is preceded by several specific ones, even if all questions are explicitly placed into the same conversational context.

To test this theoretical analysis, other respondents of the Schwarz, Strack, et al. (1991) study were asked three specific questions, pertaining to their leisuretime satisfaction, their job satisfaction, and, finally, their marital satisfaction. As shown in the second column of Table 6.1, the correlation between marital satisfaction and life satisfaction increased from $r = .32$ to $r = .46$ when answering the specific questions first brought information about one's marriage to mind. However, this increase was less pronounced than when the marital satisfaction question was the only specific question that preceded the general one ($r = .67$), reflecting that the three specific questions brought a more varied set of information to mind. This differential strength of the emerging assimilation effect is consistent with the set size predictions made by the inclusion–exclusion model (Schwarz & Bless, 1992a), as previously discussed. More importantly, introducing the three specific and the general question by a joint lead-in, thus assigning them explicitly to the same conversational context, did not reduce the emerging correlation, $r = .48$. This indicates that respondents adopted a "Taking-all-aspects-together" interpretation of the general question if it was preceded by three, rather than one, specific questions. This interpretation is further supported by a highly similar correlation of $r = .53$ when the general question was reworded to request an integrative judgment, and a highly dissimilar correlation of $r = .11$ when the reworded question required the consideration of other aspects of one's life.

In combination, these findings demonstrate that the conversational norm of nonredundancy may determine how respondents use highly accessible information in forming a judgment, resulting either in assimilation or in contrast effects. This conclusion is further supported by a study reported by Strack, Martin, and Schwarz (1988), which indicates that these effects are not restricted to order effects between similar evaluative judgments. Rather, the same variables may also affect the observed relationship between behavioral reports and subsequent judgments. Specifically, Strack et al. (1988, Experiment 2) asked U.S. college students to report their general life satisfaction as well as their dating frequency. When the life satisfaction question preceded the dating frequency question, the correlation was weak, $r = -.12$, and not significant, suggesting that dating frequency may contribute little to students' overall well-being. Reversing the question order, however, increased the correlation dramatically to $r = .66$, suggesting that dating frequency is a major contributor to life-satisfaction for college students. This reflects that the dating frequency question increased the cognitive accessibility of dating-related information, which was subsequently included in the representation formed of one's life as a whole. However, placing both questions in the same conversational context by a joint lead-in reduced the obtained correlation to nonsignificance, $r = .15$, reflecting that respondents excluded the information they had already provided when the conversational context elicited the norm of nonredundancy.

As these examples illustrate, we would draw very different conclusions about the contributions of marital satisfaction or dating frequency to overall life satisfaction, depending on the order and conversational frame in which the relevant questions are presented. Moreover, these findings challenge the popular "form-resistant correlations" notion (Stouffer & DeVinney, 1949) that holds that context effects in survey measurement are restricted to differences in means and are unlikely to affect measures of association. I return to this issue, following a discussion of differences in the means.

General and Specific Judgments: Differences in Means

As may be expected on the basis of the observed correlational differences, the interplay of cognitive and communicative processes is also likely to result in pronounced differences in the means of reported judgments. However, it is informative to consider the potential complexities of mean differences in more detail.

Table 6.2 is taken from Schwarz, Strack, and Mai (1991) and parallels the display of correlations in Table 6.1. The top panel of Table 6.2 shows the mean reported life satisfaction under conditions where the marital satisfaction question was the only specific question asked. For this analysis, respondents were separated into unhappily and happily married groups, reflecting the third of the sample reporting the lowest or highest marital satisfaction, respectively. Not surprisingly, unhappily married respondents reported lower life satisfaction than happily married respondents when the general question was asked first, as shown in the first row of Table 6.2. This difference reflects the chronic accessibility of marriage-related information. As shown in the second row, thinking about their marriage before answering the general question decreased

TABLE 6.2
Mean Differences in Life Satisfaction as a Function of Relationship Satisfaction, Question Order and Conversational Context

	Unhappily Married	Happily Married
One Specific Question		
General–specific	6.8	8.5
Specific–general	5.8	9.5
Specific–general, with joint lead-in	8.0	8.5
Three Specific Questions		
General–specific	6.8	8.5
Specific–general	7.1	9.1
Specific–general, with joint lead-in	6.7	8.9

Note. Ratings were on an 11-point scale, with 11 = *very satisfied.* Adapted from Schwarz, Strack, and Mai (1991). Reprinted by permission.

life-satisfaction for unhappily married respondents, but increased life satisfaction for happily married respondents. This indicates that the preceding marital satisfaction question increased the temporary accessibility of marriage related information. In both conditions, respondents included the chronically or temporarily accessible information about their marriage in the representation that they formed of their lives as a whole, resulting in the observed differences in general life satisfaction.

Not so, however, when the joint lead-in induced respondents to disregard information bearing on their marriage in order to avoid redundancy. In this case, the highly accessible information bearing on respondents' marriage was excluded from the representation formed and respondents presumably drew on other aspects of their lives to form the general judgment. As a result, unhappily married respondents now reported higher, and happily married respondents lower, life satisfaction than when the questions were asked in the same order without a joint lead-in, as shown in the third row of Table 6.2. Moreover, happily and unhappily married respondents no longer differed in reported general life satisfaction under this condition. This further supports the assumption that they turned to other aspects of their lives to form a general judgment, resulting in similar judgments once differences in the quality of their marriages were excluded from consideration.

Finally, as shown in the second panel of Table 6.2, no significant order effects on reported mean life satisfaction were obtained when several specific questions were asked, as would be expected on the basis of the rationale outlined in the discussion of the correlational findings.

Similar findings have been observed in other content domains. For example, Bachman and Alcser (1993) asked respondents to report their satisfaction "with the current U.S. health care system" and their satisfaction with their own health insurance plan. Most respondents who had health insurance reported high satisfaction with their own insurance plan, independently of the order in which both questions were presented (77.8% *very* or *somewhat* satisfied when the question was asked first, and 76.4% when it was asked second). Their reported satisfaction with the U.S. health care system in general, however, showed a pronounced order effect. When this question was asked first, 39.6% of the respondents reported being very or somewhat satisfied, whereas only 26.4% did so when this question was preceded by the question about their own insurance plan. Presumably, respondents who had just reported on their own health insurance plan interpreted the general question as a request for new information, much as if it were worded, "Aside from your own insurance, how satisfied are you with health insurance in the U.S. in general?" As a result, they excluded their own insurance, with which most were satisfied, from consideration when they were asked to evaluate the U.S. health care system in general, resulting in reports of lower satisfaction. Had the two questions been separated by a few filler questions, thus clouding their conversational relatedness, respondents would presumably have included information about their own insurance plan when making the general judgment, resulting in increased satisfaction (see Wänke & Schwarz, in press, for a discussion of the influence of filler items). Data bearing on this latter possibility are not available, however.

Similarly, Mason, Carlson, and Tourangeau (1994) asked respondents to report their expectations about the future development of their state economy and their local economy and presented both questions in different orders. In general, respondents were more optimistic regarding the prospects of their local than their state

economy. Reflecting this positive assessment of their local econo-
mies, 32% of the sample expected that the state economy will
improve when this was the first question asked. When the state
economy question was preceded by the local economy question,
however, only 19% expected the state economy to improve. This
presumably reflects that respondents excluded the positive information bearing on their local economy, which they had already
provided in response to the preceding question under this order
condition. Analyses of open-ended responses supported this interpretation. Specifically, respondents were asked "Why do you say
that?" after they had answered the respective questions. Content
analyses indicated that the reasons typically given for the expected
improvement of the local economy were only reported for the state
economy when the state question was asked first. When the state
question followed the local question, reasons pertaining to the local
economy were not reiterated for the state economy, much as one
would expect when respondents try to avoid redundancy in answering closely related questions.

CONCLUSIONS

In combination, the findings reviewed in this chapter emphasize
that the interpretation of related questions may change as a function
of conversational variables, resulting in markedly different responses. From a methodological perspective, these findings illustrate that a researcher may draw rather different substantive
conclusions depending on the order in which questions are asked
and the way in which related questions are introduced. Moreover,
the emerging differences are not restricted to the means or margins
of the response distribution, in contrast to what social scientists
frequently hope for. Rather, context variables may also result in
different correlational patterns, thus violating the assumption that
context effects would be restricted to differences in the means,
whereas the relationship between variables would be "form resis-
tant" (cf. Schuman & Duncan, 1974; Stouffer & DeVinney, 1949).
In fact, the data of the Schwarz, Strack, and Mai (1991) study
suggest that the opposite may often be true. Specifically, none of
the differences in mean reported life satisfaction shown in Table
6.2 can be observed when the data are analyzed without taking the
quality of respondents' marriages into account. Without separating

respondents into happily and unhappily married ones, the respective context effects cancel one another, with the moderately happily married respondents adding additional noise. As a result, no significant mean differences emerge for the sample as a whole. Although this is not surprising on theoretical grounds, it suggests that context effects in attitude measurement may often go unnoticed because their conditional nature is rarely taken into account in standard analyses (see T. Smith, 1992, for a more extended discussion of the conditionality of context effects). As the Schwarz, Strack, and Mai (1991) findings illustrate, measures of association (such as correlation coefficients) provide a more sensitive tool for detecting context effects in the overall sample than comparisons of means, provided that the variance in the data is not unduly restricted, thus limiting the possibility to observe differences in association. Obviously, the pronounced impact of question order on measures of association also implies that we would draw very different conclusions from structural equation models based on these data (see Sudman et al., 1996, chapters 4 and 5 for an extensive review of context effects in survey research and their applied implications).

From a theoretical perspective, the reviewed findings illustrate that we cannot account for the emergence of context effects on the basis of cognitive processes alone. Whereas preceding questions increase the cognitive accessibility of information used to answer them, this increase does not necessarily result in an increased use of the primed information in making subsequent judgments, in contrast to what current theorizing in social cognition would suggest. According to current models of information accessibility and use (see Bodenhausen & Wyer, 1987; Higgins & Bargh, 1987; Wyer & Srull, 1986), the use of information is determined by its accessibility in memory and its applicability to the task at hand. In all of this research, applicability has been assumed to be solely determined by the nature of the stimulus materials. As the reviewed studies indicate, however, the conversational context may change the perceived nature of the judgmental task and may lead subjects to deliberately ignore information that is easily accessible and potentially relevant to the judgment at hand. Hence, the emergence of priming effects is not only determined by the nature of the stimulus materials or the literal question asked, but also by the conversational context in which subjects are asked to make their judgment. As Strack et al. (1988) emphasized, a full understanding of the use of highly accessible information therefore requires not only a consideration of its applicability to the task at hand, but also of its appropriateness in the conversational context (see Martin & Achee, 1992; Schwarz & Bless, 1992a; Strack, 1992a, 1992b, for more general discussions of information use). Unfortunately, however, it is sometimes difficult to predict if two questions will be seen as conversationally related. In some of the studies reviewed above (Schwarz, Strack, & Mai, 1991; Strack et al., 1988), the specific and general questions were either presented on the same page of the questionnaire and introduced with a joint lead-in or were presented as the last question on one page and the first question on the next page of the same questionnaire, without a joint lead-in. Whereas these manipulations served to emphasize or cloud the relatedness of the questions asked, other studies (e.g., Bachman & Alcser, 1993; Mason et al., 1994) obtained similar effects without explicit manipulations of their conversational relatedness. Future research will need to explore features such as the similarity in question wording or response format, which may determine perceived relatedness in the absence of explicit manipulations. Without a more detailed understanding of these determinants, the theoretical insights reviewed in this chapter will remain of limited use to questionnaire designers.

7

Judgment in a Social Context: (Some) Conclusions

The cartoon presented in chapter 1 (see Fig. 1.1) portrayed research participants as isolated individuals lost in thought. The research situation, however, is better portrayed as an ongoing conversation between the researcher and research participants. Although this conversation is heavily constrained by the requirement of standardization, and may lack face-to-face contact (e.g., in questionnaire studies), it shares many of the features that characterize conversations in daily life. Most importantly, research participants bring the tacit assumptions that govern the conduct of conversation in daily life to the research situation. Hence, they expect the researcher to be a cooperative communicator, who observes the Gricean maxims of conversation and whose contributions are informative, truthful, relevant, and clear. Moreover, they design their own contributions to provide the information they infer the researcher to be interested in.

As the examples in chapter 2 illustrated, our reliance on the maxims of cooperative conversational conduct is relatively automatic and often occurs outside of conscious awareness. Thus, when A asks, "Where is Bill?" and B responds, "There's a yellow VW outside Sue's home," we do not conclude that B is switching the topic of the conversation, thus violating the maxim of relation (Levinson, 1983, p. 102). Rather, we infer that Bill has a yellow VW and that the location of the car may suggest where Bill is. In fact, the latter interpretation is so dominant that none of the students in a classroom demonstration recognized that B may be inappropriately changing the topic until made aware of this possibility. In daily life, we skillfully apply the Gricean maxims to infer a speaker's meaning and to design our own utterances. Moreover, we deliberately flout the maxims to convey nonliteral meanings, trusting that the recipient will draw the proper inferences (see chapter 2 for examples). Not so, however, when we enact the role of researcher.

As researchers, we seem to assume that the rules of conversational conduct do not apply to the research situation. This has important consequences. In designing our own contributions, we feel free to provide information that is neither informative, nor relevant, truthful, and clear, thus violating the maxims we would observe in any other context. We may do so deliberately, as in the design of experimental materials, or mindlessly, as in the unreflected use of formal features of questionnaires. Our research participants, however, have no reason to assume that the researcher is not a cooperative communicator. Hence, they go beyond the literal meaning of the researcher's contributions to determine the pragmatic meaning of the question asked and the nature of their task. At the next step, however, the researcher is likely to interpret participants' answers as if they were based solely on the *literal* rather than on the *pragmatic* meaning of the material provided to them—and finds the answers wanting.

As the examples in chapters 3 through 6 illustrated, this basic misunderstanding about the conversational nature of the research situation has contributed to some of the more surprising findings that have been treated under rubrics like "judgmental biases," "measurement errors," or "artifacts" in different fields of research. When conversational rules are observed in the research situation, or when their applicability is called into question, the respective phenomena are greatly attenuated or eliminated. Does this imply that judgmental biases are solely due to conversational violations? As emphasized repeatedly, I think the answer is a clear "No!" Like most robust phenomena, many of the biases addressed in the preceding chapters are likely to be overdetermined. If we are to identify the conditions under which they emerge in natural settings, however, we have to ensure that our experimental analogues do not elicit them for reasons that are unlikely to hold outside of our laboratories, where speakers are indeed likely to be cooperative communicators and where our real world knowledge alerts us to conditions under which they may be less than fully cooperative.

Here, I address some implications of a conversational analysis for the methodology of empirical research, our conceptualization of artifacts, and the pragmatic nature of human reasoning.

METHODOLOGICAL IMPLICATIONS

Not surprisingly, the key methodological implication of a conversational analysis of research procedures is that researchers need to be sensitive to the information that their procedures provide to participants. Of course, most researchers would claim they always are, yet their attention is usually limited to the semantic information provided, at the expense of its pragmatic implications.

This is particularly obvious when researchers want to provide "irrelevant" information in a research setting, an attempt that is extremely difficult as Kahneman and Tversky (1982) noted. Although the information may be irrelevant relative to some normative standard, the sheer fact that the experimenter presents it renders it conversationally relevant—or why else would the experimenter bother to introduce it? Hence, the "guarantee of relevance" (Sperber & Wilson, 1986) that characterizes communicated information counteracts any doubts that research participants may have based on the substantive nature of the information, rendering it likely that they will find "relevance" in whatever is presented to them. As a result, "We cannot always assume that people will or should draw the same inferences from *observing* a fact and from *being told about* the same fact" (Kahneman & Tversky, 1982, p. 504). Unfortunately, this insight is not always heeded in research on judgmental shortcomings and researchers are likely to evaluate the normative appropriateness subjects' judgments solely on the basis of the semantic, rather than the conversational, implications of the information offered to them. At the minimum, we need to check respondents' pragmatic interpretation before we conclude that they were mindlessly relying on irrelevant material (cf. Hilton, 1995, for a related discussion).

Preferably, however, we should employ procedures that do not render normatively irrelevant information conversationally relevant in the first place. In principle, this can be accomplished by conveying that the source is not a cooperative communicator. If the source is the experimenter, this strategy has the unfortunate potential of severely disrupting communication in the research situation by calling all contributions of the experimenter into question. Accordingly, this strategy requires that the crucial information is provided by a source other than the experimenter. In some studies, this has been accomplished by introducing a computer as the source or by otherwise emphasizing the random nature of the information provided, thus undermining perceived communicative intent (e.g., Schwarz, Strack, Hilton, & Naderer, 1991). As the manipulations reviewed in chapter 3 illustrate, this strategy often results in rather cumbersome experimental procedures. In other cases, researchers can rely on respondents' real world knowledge about the likely cooperative conduct of communicators. This is illustrated by the observation that misleading information does not affect eyewitness testimony when introduced by a source considered unreliable, such as the defendant's attorney in court proceedings (e.g., Dodd & Bradshaw, 1980; see chapter 4, this volume). In either case, undermining the perceived cooperativeness of the source requires considerable experimental ingenuity to overcome participants' default assumption of cooperativeness.

Note also that there is no reason to assume that the conversational relevance or normatively irrelevant information can be undermined by increasing participants' accuracy motivation. To the contrary, the more participants are motivated to arrive at the "correct" solution, the more they will try to take all the information into account that the researcher seems to deem relevant. Hence, it comes as no surprise that incentives do not decrease participants' reliance on normatively irrelevant information (Kahneman & Tversky, 1982). As Hilton (1995) noted, "incentives are not going to make respondents drop a conversationally rational interpretation in favor of a less plausible one in the context"(p. 265). Moreover, the sheer fact that an incentive for the correct solution is offered may itself convey that the solution is not obvious, thus further increasing attention to subtle, nonobvious aspects of the information provided by the researcher.

In addition to paying attention to the pragmatic information they convey in their instructions and stimulus materials, researchers also need to be aware that participants extract pertinent information from apparently formal features of the research instrument. These features include the numeric values of rating scales, the graphic layout of scales, or the nature of the response alternatives provided as part of a question. The influence of such features has often have been interpreted as evidence for "shallow responding" in survey research. From a conversational perspective, however, these phenomena are better conceptualized as reflecting the use of formal features of questionnaire design in question interpretation. Like subjects in psychological experiments, survey respondents assume that all contributions of the researcher are relevant to their task, unless marked otherwise—and the contributions of the researcher include the formal features of the questionnaire. Far from reflecting meaningless responses, the observed impact of questionnaire variables indicates that respondents as cooperative communicators draw on the context of the research conversation to infer what it is that the researcher wants to know. If so, we may expect that these effects increase with respondents' motivation, quite in contrast to what the notion of "satisficing" (Krosnick, 1991) and "shallow responding" would suggest. Unfortunately, however, questionnaire designers are often insensitive to the informational value of formal features of their questionnaires and base design decisions solely on technical convenience. To avoid surprises and misleading conclusions, it is therefore important that researchers assess what their design decisions convey to respondents. To do so, they may draw on a variety of procedures that have recently been developed to explore respondents' understanding of survey questions (see the contributions to Schwarz & Sudman, 1996, and chapter 2 of Sudman et al., 1996). These procedures include think-aloud protocols, paraphrasing tasks, and the interpretation of answers that have allegedly been given by other participants in response to questions that differ in relevant design features.

Finally, the rules of cooperative conversational conduct do not only influence what research participants infer from the information provided to them, but also influence which information participants are likely to provide to the researcher. Specifically, research participants as cooperative communicators try to be informative and to provide new information, rather than information that the researcher already has. Hence, they interpret repeated, or highly similar, questions as a request for new information. As reviewed in chapter 6, these shifts in question interpretation may result in apparent inconsistencies or "errors" across the question sequence (as illustrated by conversational analyses of Piagetian conservation tasks) and in unique context effects in attitude measurement. Importantly, these shifts in question meaning are not obtained when the repeated question is posed by a communicator who was not the recipient of the initial answer, thus eliminating any concerns about redundancy (e.g., Strack et al., 1991).

This aspect of cooperative conduct has potentially important methodological implications for the "two-experiments" paradigm, which is often employed to reduce demand effects in experiments. Specifically, researchers often separate the experimental manipulation and the assessment of its expected impact by making subjects believe that they participate in two unrelated experiments, conducted by two different researchers. This procedure deliberately disrupts the context in which the manipulation was administered in order to disguise the relationship between the manipulation and the dependent measures. Although this procedure does reduce possible demand effects, it also changes the nature of the communicative context, including which information may or may not be considered redundant with information provided earlier. Hence, the observation that the same manipulation has different effects when the dependent measures are assessed as part of the "same" or a "different" experiment may reflect the differential operation of demand effects as well as changes in the pragmatic meaning of the questions asked.

Throughout, a conversational analysis of research procedures highlights that the meaning that the researcher wants to convey is not necessarily the meaning that research participants infer. Although this fallibility characterizes all human communication, its potential is exaggerated in research situations where standardized procedures preclude the feedback and correction available in other situations and where researchers do not observe the rules of cooperative conduct. Accordingly, special care needs to be taken to understand participants' interpretation of their task, unless we want to run the risk of misinterpreting faulty communication as faulty cognition.

ARTIFACTS IN SOCIAL RESEARCH

Obviously, researchers have long been aware that research procedures may have unintended "side effects" and it is informative to review this research from a conversational perspective (see Bless, Strack, & Schwarz, 1993, for more detail). Stimulated by Orne's (1962, 1969) seminal discussion of demand characteristics, researchers have paid considerable attention to the emergence of artifacts in experimental research, addressing what has often been called the *social psychology* of the psychological experiment (see Kruglanski, 1975, for an overview). This research portrayed experiments as unique endeavors that differ in important ways from social interaction in daily life. Central to Orne's (1962, 1969) analysis was the assumption that subjects have "an emotional investment in research which stems from three goals: to further scientific knowledge, to find out something about him- or herself; and to present him- or herself in a positive light" (Kihlstrom, 1995, p. 11). To attain these goals, they enter into an implicit contractual arrangement with the experimenter that implies that they will "play along" with the experiment and that the experimenter guarantees that they will not suffer any harm. Enacting the role of "good subject," research participants look for cues in the experimental situation that provide them with the experimenter's hypothesis and tailor their behavior accordingly. As Kihlstrom (1995) noted, Orne "thought that demand characteristics were a problem because of motives—to help the experimenter, to learn about themselves, and to look good—that *were peculiar to research participants*" (p. 23, italics added). Consistent with this emphasis, research in this tradition focused on subjects' motivation rather than the processes by which subjects extract information from experimental procedures.

In contrast, a conversational analysis suggests that we do not need to make special assumptions about specific motives germane to the research situation. Rather, the examples reviewed in the preceding chapters indicate that subjects' behavior in an experiment or research interview is guided by the same assumptions and motivations that govern the conduct of conversation in any other setting (see Bless et al., 1993; Kihlstrom, 1995, for comparisons of Orne's analysis and a conversational perspective). From a conversational point of view, the key difference between experiments and conversations in natural settings is only that the experimenter is less likely to comply with conversational rules in conducting an experiment than in conducting any other conversation, while subjects have no reason to suspect so. Hence, they apply the tacit assumptions that govern the conduct of conversation to the research setting and go beyond the literal information provided to them by drawing inferences on the basis of the conversational context. From this perspective, so called "artifacts" do not reflect that participation in an experiment elicits unusual behavior—to the contrary, it is exactly subjects' reliance on the usual rules of conduct that is at the heart of the phenomena just reviewed: "In that respect, at least, Orne needn't have worried, for what happens in the laboratory is entirely representative of what goes on in the real world," as Kihlstrom (1995, p. 23) concluded.

THINKING IS FOR DOING

Finally, it is appropriate to consider the relevance of Grice's cooperative principle in a broader context. After two decades of research that focused on shortcomings in social judgment, researchers have recently emphasized that "people are good enough perceivers" (Fiske, 1992, p. 879). Drawing on James' (1890/1983) pragmatism, Fiske noted in a review of social perception research that "a pragmatic perspective argues . . . that people are no fools; they use workable strategies with adequate outcomes for their own purposes. The pragmatic perceiver does not necessarily maximize accuracy, efficiency, or adaptability; *good enough understanding*, given his or her goals, is the rule" (p. 879, italics added). Indeed, an abundant body of research illustrates how social perception is shaped by perceivers' goals and is often "good enough" for the goal at hand, even under conditions where social perception falls short of normative standards that do not take the perceiver's goals into account (see Fiske, 1992, 1993, for reviews).

An analysis of human cognition based on the pragmatic assumption that thinking is for doing, is highly compatible with the conversational perspective offered here and needs to take Grice's (1975) cooperative principle into account. As noted in chapter 2, the applicability of the cooperative principle extends beyond the realm of conversations, as Grice emphasized. In his view, the maxims of cooperative conduct are rational rules that apply to all situations that require cooperation, as one of Grice's examples may illustrate. When mixing the ingredients for a cake, for instance, we do not expect to be handed a good book (maxim of relation), nor do we want to receive salt when we ask for sugar (maxim of quality), or to be handed four spoons when we need one (maxim of quantity). And when we ask for the amount of sugar needed, we expect a quantitative answer, not an obscure riddle (maxim of manner). Although examples of this type seem utterly obvious and trivial, it is exactly their obviousness that illustrates to what extent we rely on rules of cooperative conduct in getting things done. In fact, relying on these rules as a default serves us well in most circumstances. Moreover, our application of these rules is automatic and unless indicated otherwise, we assume that the other is cooperative and interpret apparent deviations based on this assumption. In making such inferences, we go beyond the semantic information given and draw on the conversational implicatures in addition to the logical implications of the utterance. The inferences we arrive at are systematic and predictable rather than ad hoc. Moreover, they are likely to be correct if the speaker *is* cooperative—and if we get it wrong, the speaker can correct us. By and large, our default reliance on Gricean maxims is a rational and efficient way to "get things done" and adherence to the maxims facilitates smooth and efficient interaction.

Reliance on the cooperative principle leads us astray, however, when the speaker is not cooperative and/or the situation does not allow for the correction of erroneous inferences. As noted repeatedly, both features hold for many research situations. As a result, subjects form representations of their task based on the logical implications as well as the conversational implicatures of the information provided to them and may try to "get something done" that the experimenter didn't want them to do (while implicating otherwise). Yet, the researcher evaluates their judgment relative to normative models that draw only on the logical implications and finds it lacking. As Funder (1987) noted in a related context, "it seems ironic that going beyond the information given. . . is so often interpreted by social psychologists as symptomatic of flawed judgment. Current thinking in the field of artificial intelligence is that this propensity is exactly what makes people smarter than computers"(p. 82). To understand this special potential of human information processors, we need to pay closer attention to the social context of human judgment and cognition. Taking the tacit assumptions that govern the conduct of conversation into account provides a promising starting point for this endeavor.

REFERENCES

Bachman, G., & Alcser, K. (1993). *Limitations of conventional polling methods in studying attitudes about health care in america: An example of question sequence effects.* Unpublished manuscript: University of Michigan, Ann Arbor.

Billiet, J., Loosveldt, G., & Waterplas, L. (1988). *Response-effecten bij survey-vragen in het Nederlands taalgebied* [Response effects in survey questions in Dutch speaking countries]. Leuven, Belgium: Katholieke Universiteit.

Bishop, G., Hippler, H. J., Schwarz, N., & Strack, F. (1988). A comparison of response effects in self-administered and telephone surveys. In R. M. Groves, P. Biemer, L. Lyberg, J. T. Massey, W. L. Nicholls, & J. Waksberg (Eds.), *Telephone survey methodology* (pp. 321–340). New York: Wiley.

Bishop, G. F., Oldendick, R. W., & Tuchfarber, L. A. J. (1983). Effects of filter questions in public opinion surveys. *Public Opinion Quarterly, 47,* 528–546.

Bishop, G. F., Oldendick, R. W., & Tuchfarber, L. A. J. (1986). Opinions on fictitious issues: the pressure to answer survey questions. *Public Opinion Quarterly, 50,* 240–250.

Bless, H., Bohner, G., Hild, T., & Schwarz, N. (1992). Asking difficult questions: Task complexity increases the impact of response alternatives. *European Journal of Social Psychology, 22,* 309–312.

Bless, H., Strack, F., & Schwarz, N. (1993). The informative functions of research procedures: Bias and the logic of conversation. *European Journal of Social Psychology, 23,* 149–165.

Bodenhausen, G. V., & Wyer, R. S. (1987). Social cognition and social reality: Information acquisition and use in the laboratory and the real world. In H. J. Hippler, N. Schwarz, & S. Sudman (Eds.), *Social information processing and survey methodology* (pp. 6–41). New York: Springer Verlag.

Bradburn, N. M. (1982). Question wording effects in surveys. In R. Hogarth (Ed.), *Question framing and response consistency* (pp. 65–76). San Francisco: Jossey-Bass.

Bradburn, N. M. (1983). Response effects. In P. H. Rossi, & J. D. Wright (Eds.), *The handbook of survey research* (pp. 289–328). New York: Academic Press.

Bradburn, N. M., Rips, L. J., & Shevell, S. K. (1987). Answering autobiographical questions: The impact of memory and inference on surveys. *Science, 236,* 157–161.

Clark, H. H. (1977). Inferences in comprehension. In D. La Berge, & S. Samuels, (Eds.), *Basic processes in reading: Perception and comprehension* (pp. 243–263). Hillsdale, NJ: Lawrence Erlbaum Associates.

Clark, H. H. (1985). Language use and language users. In G. Lindzey & E. Aronson (Eds.), *Handbook of social psychology* (Vol. 2, pp. 179–232). New York: Random House.

Clark, H. H., & Brennan, S. E. (1991). Grounding in communication. In L. Resnick, J. Levine, & S. D. Teasley (Eds.), *Perspectives on socially shared cognition* (pp. 127–149). Washington, DC: American Psychological Association.

Clark, H. H., & Clark, E. V. (1977). *Psychology and language.* New York: Harcourt, Brace, Jovanovich.

Clark, H. H., & Haviland, S. E. (1977). Comprehension and the given-new contract. In R. O. Freedle (Ed.), *Discourse production and comprehension* (pp. 1–40). Hillsdale, NJ: Lawrence Erlbaum Associates.

Clark, H. H., & Schober, M. F. (1992). Asking questions and influencing answers. In J. M. Tanur (Ed.), *Questions about questions* (pp. 15–48). New York: Russell Sage.

Clark, H. H., Schreuder, R., & Buttrick, S. (1983). Common ground and the understanding of demonstrative reference. *Journal of Verbal Learning and Verbal Behavior, 22,* 245–258.

Converse, P. E. (1964). The nature of belief systems in mass politics. In D. Apter (Ed.), *Ideology and discontent* (pp. 238–45). New York: The Free Press.

Converse, P. E. (1970). Attitudes and non-attitudes: Continuation of a dialogue. In E. R. Tufte (Ed.), *The quantitative analysis of social problems* (pp. 188–189). Reading, MA: Addison-Wesley.

Dawes, R. M., & Smith, T. (1985). Attitude and opinion measurement. In G. Lindzey & E. Aronson (Eds.), *Handbook of social psychology* (Vol. 2, pp. 509–566). New York: Random House.

Dockrell, J., Neilson, I., & Campbell, R. (1980). Conservation accidents revisited. *International Journal of Behavioral Development, 3,* 423–439.

Dodd, D. H., & Bradshaw, J. M. (1980). Leading questions and memory: Pragmatic constraints. *Journal of Verbal Learning and Verbal Behavior, 19,* 695–704.

Donaldson, M. (1982). Conservation: What is the question? *British Journal of Psychology, 73,* 199–207.

Elbers, E. (1986). Interaction and instruction in the conservation experiment. *European Journal of Psychology of Education, 1,* 77–89.

Erikson, R. S., Luttberg, N. R., & Tedin, K. T. (1988). *American public opinion* (3rd ed.). New York: Macmillan.

Fischhoff, B., Slovic, P., & Lichtenstein, S. (1979). Subjective sensitivity analysis. *Organizational Behavior and Human Performance, 23,* 339–359.

Fiske, S. T. (1992). Thinking is for doing: Portraits of social cognition from daguerreotype to laserphoto. *Journal of Personality and Social Psychology, 63,* 877–889.

Fiske, S. T. (1993). Social cognition and social perception. *Annual Review of Psychology, 44,* 155–194.

Funder, D. C. (1987). Errors and mistakes: Evaluating the accuracy of social judgment. *Psychological Bulletin, 101,* 75–90.

Fussel, S. R., & Krauss, R. M. (1989a). Understanding friends and strangers: the effects of audience design on message comprehension. *European Journal of Social Psychology, 19,* 509–525.

Fussel, S. R., & Krauss, R. M. (1989b). The effects of intended audience on message production and comprehension: reference in a common ground framework. *Journal of Experimental Social Psychology, 25,* 203–219.

Gaskell, G. D., O'Muircheartaigh, C. A., & Wright, D. B. (1994). Survey questions about the frequency of vaguely defined events: The effects of response alternatives. *Public Opinion Quarterly, 58,* 241–254.

Gaskell, G. D., O'Muircheartaigh, C. A., & Wright, D. B. (1995). *How response alternatives affect different kinds of behavioural frequency questions.* Unpublished manuscript, London School of Economics, London, UK.

Ginossar, Z., & Trope, Y. (1987). Problem solving and judgment under uncertainty. *Journal of Personality and Social Psychology, 52,* 464–474.

Grayson, C. E., & Schwarz, N. (1995). *When "rarely" is "never": The numeric value of rating scales and the interpretation of scale labels.* Manuscript submitted for review.

Grice, H. P. (1975). Logic and conversation. In P. Cole & J. L. Morgan (Eds.), *Syntax and semantics, 3: Speech acts* (pp. 41–58). New York: Academic Press.

Grice, H. P. (1978). Further notes on logic and conversation. In P. Cole (Ed.), *Syntax and semantics, 9: Pragmatics* (pp. 113–128). New York: Academic Press.

Gruenfeld, D. H., & Wyer, R. S. (1992). Semantics and pragmatics of social influence: How affirmations and denials affect beliefs in referent propositions. *Journal of Personality and Social Psychology, 62,* 38–49.

Hargreaves, D. J., Molloy, C. G., & Pratt, A. R. (1982). Social factors in conservation. *British Journal of Psychology, 73,* 231–234.

Harris, R. J., & Monaco, G. E. (1978). Psychology of pragmatic implication: Information processing between the lines. *Journal of Experimental Psychology: General, 107,* 1–27.

Haviland, S., & Clark, H. (1974). What's new? Acquiring new information as a process in comprehension. *Journal of Verbal Learning and Verbal Behavior, 13,* 512–521.

Higgins, E. T. (1981). The "communication game": Implications for social cognition and communication. In E. T. Higgins, M. P. Zanna, & C. P. Herman (Eds.), *Social cognition: The Ontario Symposium* (Vol. 1, pp. 343–392). Hillsdale, NJ: Lawrence Erlbaum Associates.

Higgins, E. T., & Bargh, J. A. (1987). Social cognition and social perception. *Annual Review of Psychology, 38,* 369–425.

Higgins, E. T., Fondacaro, R. A., & McCann, C. D. (1982). Rules and roles: The "communication game" and speaker–listener processes. In W. P. Dickson (Ed.), *Children's oral communication skills* (pp. 289–312). New York: Academic Press.

Hilton, D. J. (1995). The social context of reasoning: Conversational inference and rational judgment. *Psychological Bulletin, 118,* 248–271.

Hippler, H. J., & Schwarz, N. (1989). "No opinion" filters: A cognitive perspective. *International Journal of Public Opinion Research, 1,* 77–87.

James, W. (1890/1983). *The principles of psychology.* Cambridge, MA: Harvard University Press. (Original work published 1890).

Jones, E. E. (1990). *Interpersonal perception.* New York: Freeman.

Jones, E. E., & Harris, V. A. (1967). The attribution of attitudes. *Journal of Experimental Social Psychology, 3,* 1–24.

Kahneman, D., Slovic, P., & Tversky, A. (1982). *Judgment under uncertainty: Heuristics and biases.* Cambridge, UK: Cambridge University Press.

Kahneman, D., & Tversky, A. (1973). On the psychology of prediction. *Psychological Review, 80,* 237–251.

Kahneman, D., & Tversky, A. (1982). On the study of statistical intuitions. In D. Kahneman, P. Slovic, & A. Tversky (Eds.), *Judgment under uncertainty: Heuristics and biases* (pp. 493–508). Cambridge, UK: Cambridge University Press.

Kihlstrom, J. F. (1995, June). *From the subject's point of view: The experiment as conversation and collaboration between investigator and subject.* Invited address presented at the meetings of the American Psychological Society, New York.

Kohlberg, L., & Ullian, D. Z. (1974). Stages in the development of psychosexual concepts and attitudes. In R. C. Friedman, R. M. Richart, & R. L. Van de Wiele (Eds.), *Sex differences in behavior* (pp. 209–222). New York: Wiley.

Krauss, R. M., & Fussel, S. R. (1991). Perspective-taking in communication: Representations of others' knowledge in reference. *Social Cognition, 9,* 2–24.

Krosnick, J. A. (1991). Response strategies for coping with the cognitive demands of attitude measures in surveys. *Applied Cognitive Psychology, 5,* 213–236.

Krosnick, J. A., Li, F., & Lehman, D. R. (1990). Conversational conventions, order of information acquisition, and the effect of base rates and individuating information on social judgment. *Journal of Personality and Social Psychology, 59,* 1140–1152.

Kruglanski, A. W. (1975). The human subject in the psychology experiment: Fact and artifact. In L. Berkowitz (Ed.), *Advances in experimental social psychology* (Vol. 8, pp. 101–147). New York: Academic Press.

Lakoff, R. (1975). *Language and a woman's place*. New York: Harper & Row.

Levinson, S. C. (1983). *Pragmatics*. Cambridge, UK: Cambridge University Press.

Light, P., Buckingham, N., & Robbins, A. H. (1979). The conservation task as an interactional setting. *British Journal of Educational Psychology, 49*, 304–310.

Loftus, E. F. (1975). Leading questions and the eyewitness report. *Cognitive Psychology, 7*, 560–572.

Loftus, E. F. (1979). *Eyewitness testimony*. Cambridge, MA: Harvard University Press.

Lombardi, W. J., Higgins, E. T., & Bargh, J. A. (1987). The role of consciousness in priming effects on categorization: Assimilation and contrast as a function of awareness of the priming task. *Personality and Social Psychology Bulletin, 13*, 411–429.

Markus, H., & Zajonc, R. B. (1985). The cognitive perspective in social psychology. In G. Lindzey, & E. Aronson (Eds.), *The handbook of social psychology* (Vol.1, pp. 137–230). New York: Random House.

Martin, L. L., & Achee, J. W. (1992). Beyond accessibility: The role of processing objectives in judgment. In L. L. Martin & A. Tesser (Eds.), *The construction of social judgments* (pp. 195–216). Hillsdale, NJ: Lawrence Erlbaum Associates.

Martin, L. L., & Clark, L. F. (1990). Social cognition: Exploring the mental processes involved in human social interaction. In M. W. Eysenck (Ed.), *Cognitive psychology: An international review* (pp. 265–310). Chichester: Wiley.

Mason, R., Carlson, J. E., & Tourangeau, R. (1994). Contrast effects and subtraction in part-whole questions. *Public Opinion Quarterly, 58*, 569–578.

McCann, C. D., & Higgins, E. T. (1992). Personal and contextual factors in communication: A review of the "communication game." In G. R. Semin & K. Fiedler (Eds.), *Language, interaction, and social cognition* (pp. 144–172). Newbury Park, CA: Sage.

McGarrigle, J., & Donaldson, M. (1974). Conservation accidents. *Cognition, 3*, 341–350.

Menon, G. (1994). Judgments of behavioral frequencies: Memory search and retrieval strategies. In N. Schwarz & S. Sudman, S. (Eds.), *Autobiographi-*

cal memory and the validity of retrospective reports (pp. 161–172). New York: Springer Verlag.

Menon, G., Rahgubir, P., & Schwarz, N. (1995). Behavioral frequency judgments: An accessibility–diagnosticity framework. *Journal of Consumer Research, 22,* 212–228.

Miller, A. G., Schmidt, D., Meyer, C., & Colella, A. (1984). The perceived value of constrained behavior: Pressures toward biased inference in the attitude attribution paradigm. *Social Psychology Quarterly, 47,* 160–171.

Molenaar, N. J. (1982). Response effects of formal charactersitics of questions. In W. Dijkstra & J. van der Zouwen (Eds.), *Response behavior in the survey interview* (pp. 49–90). New York: Academic Press.

Nisbett, R. E., & Borgida, E. (1975). Attribution and the psychology of prediction. *Journal of Personality and Social Psychology, 32,* 932–943.

Nisbett, R. E., & Ross, L. (1980). *Human inference: Strategies and shortcomings of social judgment.* New York: Prentice Hall.

Orne, M. T. (1962). On the social psychology of the psychological experiment: With particular reference to demand characteristics and their implications. *American Psychologist, 17,* 776–783.

Orne, M. T. (1969). Demand characteristics and the concept of quasi-controls. In R. Rosenthal & R. L. Rosnow (Eds.), *Artifact in behavioral research* (pp. 143–179). New York: Academic Press.

Piaget, J. (1952). *The child's conception of number.* London, UK: Routledge & Kegan Paul.

Piaget, J., & Inhelder, B. (1969). *The psychology of the child.* New York: Basic Books.

Prince, E. F. (1981). Towards a taxonomy of given-new information. In P. Cole (Ed.), *Radical pragmatics* (pp. 223–256). New York: Academic Press.

Rose, S. A., & Blank, M. (1974). The potency of context in children's cognition: An illustration through conservation. *Child Development, 45,* 499–502.

Ross, L. (1977). The intuitive psychologist and his shortcomings: Distortion in the attribution process. In L. Berkowitz (Ed.), *Advances in experimental social psychology* (Vol. 10, pp. 174–221). New York: Academic Press.

Ross, L., & Nisbett, R. E. (1991). *The person and the situation.* New York: McGraw-Hill.

Schiffer, S. (1972). *Meaning*. Oxford, UK: Clarendon Press.

Schuman, H. (1986). Ordinary questions, survey questions, and policy questions. *Public Opinion Quarterly, 50*, 432–442.

Schuman, H., & Duncan, O. D. (1974). Questions about attitude survey questions. In H. L. Costner (Ed.), *Sociological methodology*. San Francisco: Jossey-Bass.

Schuman, H., & Kalton, G. (1985). Survey methods. In G. Lindzey, & E. Aronson (Eds.), *Handbook of social psychology* (Vol. I, pp. 635–698). New York: Random House

Schuman, H., & Presser, S. (1977). Question wording as an independent variable in survey analysis. *Sociological Methods and Research, 6*, 151–176.

Schuman, H., & Presser, S. (1981). *Questions and answers in attitude surveys*. New York: Academic Press.

Schwarz, N. (1987). *Stimmung als Information. Untersuchungen zum Einfluß von Stimmungen auf die Bewertung des eigenen Lebens*. [Mood as information. The impact of moods on the evaluation of one's life.]. Heidelberg: Springer Verlag.

Schwarz, N. (1990). Assessing frequency reports of mundane behaviors: Contributions of cognitive psychology to questionnaire construction. In C. Hendrick & M. S. Clark (Eds.), *Research methods in personality and social psychology (Review of Personality and Social Psychology, 11*, 98–119). Beverly Hills, CA: Sage.

Schwarz, N. (1996). *Misleading by asserting the truth*. Unpublished research, University of Michigan, Ann Arbor.

Schwarz, N., & Bienias, J. (1990). What mediates the impact of response alternatives on frequency reports of mundane behaviors? *Applied Cognitive Psychology, 4*, 61–72.

Schwarz, N., & Bless, H. (1992a). Constructing reality and its alternatives: An inclusion/exclusion model of assimilation and contrast effects in social judgment. In L. Martin & A. Tesser (Eds.), *The construction of social judgment* (pp. 217–245). Hillsdale, NJ: Lawrence Erlbaum Associates.

Schwarz, N., & Bless, H. (1992b). Scandals and the public's trust in politicians: Assimilation and contrast effects. *Personality and Social Psychology Bulletin, 18*, 574–579.

Schwarz, N., Bless, H., Bohner, G., Harlacher, U., & Kellenbenz, M. (1991). Response scales as frames of reference: The impact of frequency range on diagnostic judgment. *Applied Cognitive Psychology, 5*, 37–50.

Schwarz, N., Grayson, C. E., Knäuper, B., & Wänke, M. (1996, May). *Rating scales and question interpretation: When the numbers and graphics tell you what the words don't.* Paper presented at the annual meeting of the American Association for Public Opinion Research, Salt Lake City, UT.

Schwarz, N., & Hippler, H. J. (1987). What response scales may tell your respondents: Informative functions of response alternatives. In H. J. Hippler, N. Schwarz, & S. Sudman (Eds.), *Social information processing and survey methodology* (pp. 163–178). New York: Springer Verlag.

Schwarz, N., & Hippler, H. J. (1990). *The informational value of frequency scales.* Unpublished research, ZUMA, Mannheim, Germany.

Schwarz, N., & Hippler, H. J. (1991). Response alternatives: The impact of their choice and ordering. In P. Biemer, R. Groves, N. Mathiowetz, & S. Sudman (Eds.), *Measurement error in surveys* (pp. 41–56). Chichester, UK: Wiley.

Schwarz, N., & Hippler, H. J. (1992). *Context effects and questionnaire layout.* Unpublished research, ZUMA, Mannheim, Germany.

Schwarz, N., & Hippler, H. J. (1995). The numeric values of rating scales: A comparison of their impact in mail surveys and telephone interviews. *International Journal of Public Opinion Research, 7,* 72–74.

Schwarz, N., Hippler, H. J., & Noelle-Neumann, E. (1994). Retrospective reports: The impact of response alternatives. In N. Schwarz & S. Sudman (Eds.), *Autobiographical memory and the validity of retrospective reports* (pp. 187–199). NY: Springer Verlag.

Schwarz, N., Hippler, H.J., Deutsch, B., & Strack, F. (1985). Response scales: Effects of category range on reported behavior and subsequent judgments. *Public Opinion Quarterly, 49,* 388–395.

Schwarz, N., Knäuper, B., Hippler, H. J., Noelle-Neumann, E., & Clark, L. F. (1991). Rating scales: Numeric values may change the meaning of scale labels. *Public Opinion Quarterly, 55,* 570–582.

Schwarz, N., & Scheuring, B. (1988). Judgments of relationship satisfaction: Inter- and intraindividual comparison strategies as a function of questionnaire structure. *European Journal of Social Psychology, 18,* 485–496.

Schwarz, N., & Scheuring, B. (1991). Die Erfassung gesundheitsrelevanten Verhaltens: Kognitionspsychologische Aspekte und methodologische Implikationen [The assessment of health relevant behaviors: Cognitive processes and methodological implications]. In

J. Haisch (Ed.), *Gesundheitspsychologie* (pp. 47–63). Heidelberg, FRG: Asanger.

Schwarz, N., & Scheuring, B. (1992). Selbstberichtete Verhaltens-und Symptomhäufigkeiten: Was Befragte aus Anwortvorgaben des Fragebogens lernen. [Frequency reports of psychosomatic symptoms: What respondents learn from response alternatives]. *Zeitschrift für Klinische Psychologie, 22,* 197–208.

Schwarz, N., & Strack, F. (1991). Evaluating one's life: A judgment model of subjective well-being. In F. Strack, M. Argyle, & N. Schwarz (Eds.), *Subjective well-being. An interdisciplinary perspective* (pp. 27–47). Oxford: Pergamon.

Schwarz, N., Strack, F., Hilton, D. J., & Naderer, G. (1991). Judgmental biases and the logic of conversation: The contextual relevance of irrelevant information. *Social Cognition, 9,* 67–84.

Schwarz, N., Strack, F., Hippler, H. J., & Bishop, G. (1991). The impact of administration mode on response effects in survey measurement. *Applied Cognitive Psychology, 5,* 193–212.

Schwarz, N., Strack, F., & Mai, H. P. (1991). Assimilation and contrast effects in part-whole question sequences: A conversational logic analysis. *Public Opinion Quarterly, 55,* 3–23.

Schwarz, N., Strack, F., Müller, G., & Chassein, B. (1988). The range of response alternatives may determine the meaning of the question: Further evidence on informative functions of response alternatives. *Social Cognition, 6,* 107–117.

Schwarz, N., & Sudman, S. (Eds.). (1996). *Answering questions: Methodology for determining cognitive and communicative processes in survey research.* San Francisco: Jossey-Bass.

Siegal, M., Waters, L. J., & Dinwiddy, L. S. (1988). Misleading children: Causal attributions for inconsistency under repeated questioning. *Journal of Experimental Child Psychology, 45,* 438–456.

Slaby, R. G., & Frey, K. S. (1975). Development of gender constancy and selective attention to same-sex models. *Child Development, 20,* 691–696.

Smetana, J. G., & Letourneau, K. J. (1984). Development of gender constancy and children's sex-typed free play behavior. *Child Development, 20,* 691–696.

Smith, T. W. (1992). Thoughts on the nature of context effects. In N. Schwarz & S. Sudman (Eds.), *Context effects in social and psychological research* (pp. 163–185). New York: Springer Verlag.

Smith, T. W. (1995, May). Little things matter: A sampler of how differences in questionnaire format can affect survey responses. Paper presented at the annual meeting of the American Association for Public Opinion Research, Ft. Lauderdale, FL.

Smith, V., & Ellsworth, P. C. (1987). The social psychology of eyewitness accuracy: Leading questions and communicator expertise. *Journal of Applied Psychology, 72,* 292–300.

Sperber, D., & Wilson, D. (1981). Pragmatics. *Cognition, 10,* 281–286.

Sperber, D., & Wilson, D. (1986). *Relevance: Communication and cognition.* Cambridge, MA: Harvard University Press.

Stalnaker, R. C. (1978). Assertion. In P. Cole (Ed.), *Syntax and semantics, Vol. 9: Pragmatics* (pp. 315–332). New York: Academic Press.

Stouffer, S. A., & DeVinney, L. C. (1949). How personal adjustment varied in the army—by background characteristics of the soldiers. In S. A. Stouffer, E. A. Suchman, L. C. DeVinney, S. A. Star, & R. M. Williams (Eds.), *The American soldier: Adjustment during army life* (pp. 123–144). Princeton, NJ: Princeton University Press.

Strack, F. (1992a). Order effects in survey research: Activative and informative functions of preceding questions. In N. Schwarz & S. Sudman (Eds.), *Context effects in social and psychological research* (pp. 23–34). New York: Springer Verlag.

Strack, F. (1992b). The different routes to social judgments: Experiential versus informational strategies. In L. Martin & A. Tesser (Eds.), *The construction of social judgment* (pp. 249–275). Hillsdale, NJ: Lawrence Erlbaum Associates.

Strack, F. (1994a). *Zur Psychologie der standardisierten Befragung: Kognitive und kommunikative Prozesse* [The psychology of standardized interviews: Cognitive and communicative processes]. Heidelberg, FRG: Springer Verlag.

Strack, F. (1994b). Response processes in social judgment. In R. S. Wyer & T. K. Srull (Eds.), *Handbook of social cognition* (2nd ed., Vol. 1, pp. 287–322). Hillsdale, NJ: Lawrence Erlbaum Associates.

Strack, F., & Martin, L. (1987). Thinking, judging, and communicating: A process account of context effects in attitude surveys. In H. J. Hippler, N. Schwarz, & S. Sudman (Eds.), *Social information processing and survey methodology* (pp. 123–148). New York: Springer Verlag.

Strack, F., Martin, L. L., & Schwarz, N. (1988). Priming and communication: The social determinants of information use in judgments of life-satisfaction. *European Journal of Social Psychology, 18,* 429–442.

Strack, F., & Schwarz, N. (1992). Communicative influences in standardized question situations: The case of implicit collaboration. In K. Fiedler & G. Semin (Eds.), *Language, interaction and social cognition* (pp. 173–193). Beverly Hills, CA: Sage.

Strack, F., Schwarz, N., Bless, H., Kübler, A., & Wänke, M. (1993). Awareness of the influence as a determinant of assimilation versus contrast. *European Journal of Social Psychology, 23*, 53–62.

Strack, F., Schwarz, N., & Gschneidinger, E. (1985). Happiness and reminiscing: The role of time perspective, mood, and mode of thinking. *Journal of Personality and Social Psychology, 49*, 1460–1469.

Strack, F., Schwarz, N., & Wänke, M. (1991). Semantic and pragmatic aspects of context effects in social and psychological research. *Social Cognition, 9*, 111–125.

Sudman, S., Bradburn, N., & Schwarz, N. (1996). *Thinking about answers: The application of cognitive processes to survey methodology.* San Francisco, CA: Jossey-Bass.

Swann, W. B., Giuliano, T., & Wegner, D. M. (1982). Where leading questions can lead: The power of conjecture in social interaction. *Journal of Personality and Social Psychology, 42*, 1025–1035.

Tetlock, P. E., & Boettger, R. (1989). Accountability: A social magnifier of the dilusion effect. *Journal of Personality and Social Psychology, 57*, 388–398.

Tourangeau, R. (1984). Cognitive science and survey methods: A cognitive perspective. In T. Jabine, M. Straf, J. Tanur, & R. Tourangeau (Eds.), *Cognitive aspects of survey methodology: Building a bridge between disciplines* (pp. 73–100). Washington, DC: National Academy Press.

Trometer, R. (1994). *Warum sind Befragte "meingungslos"? Kognitive und kommunikative Prozesse im Interview* [Why are respondents without an opinion? Cognitive and communicative processes in survey interviews]. Unpublished doctoral dissertation, University of Mannheim, Germany.

Trope, Y., & Ginossar, Z. (1988). On the use of statistical and non-statistical knowledge: A problem-solving approach. In D. Bar-Tal & A. W. Kruglanski (Eds.), *The social psychology of knowledge* (pp. 209–230). New York: Cambridge University Press.

Turner, C. F., & Martin, E. (Eds.). (1984). *Surveying subjective phenomena* (Vol. 1). New York: Russel Sage.

Tversky, A., & Kahneman, D. (1983). Extensional versus intuitive reasoning: The conjunction fallacy in probability judgment. *Psychological Review, 90,* 293–315.

Wänke, M., & Schwarz, N. (in press). Context effects in attitude measurement: The operation of buffer items. In L. Lyberg, P. Biemer, M. Collins, E. DeLeeuw, C. Dippo, & N. Schwarz (Eds.), *Survey measurement and process quality.* Chichester, UK: Wiley.

Wegner, D. M., Wenzlaff, R., Kerker, R. M., & Beattie, A. E. (1981). Incrimination through innuendo: Can media questions become public answers? *Journal of Personality and Social Psychology, 40,* 822–832.

Woll, S. B., Weeks, D. G., Fraps, C. L., Pendergrass, J., & Vanderplas, M. A. (1980). Role of sentence context in the encoding of trait descriptors. *Journal of Personality and Social Psychology, 39,* 59–68.

Wright, E. F., & Wells, G. L. (1988). Is the attitude-attribution paradigm suitable for investigating the dispositional bias? *Personality and Social Psychology Bulletin, 14,* 183–190.

Wyer, R. S., & Gruenfeld, D. H. (1995). Information processing in social contexts: Implications for social memory and judgment. In M. Zanna (Ed.), *Advances in experimental social psychology* (Vol. 27, pp. 49–89). San Diego, CA: Academic Press.

Wyer, R. S., & Srull, T. K. (1986). Human cognition in its social context. *Psychological Review, 93,* 322–359.

Zukier, H. A., & Pepitone, A. (1984). Social roles and strategies in prediction: Some determinants in the use of base-rate information. *Journal of Personality and Social Psychology, 47,* 349–360.

Author Index

G

Gaskell, G. D., 50, 52
Ginossar, Z., 18, 23
Giuliano, T., 38
Grayson, C. E., 45
Grice, H. P., 4, 7, 8, 11, 90
Gruenfeld, D. H., 39
Gschneidinger, E., 71

H

Hargreaves, D. J., 66
Harlacher, U., 4, 53
Harris, R. J., 39
Harris, V. A., 3, 28
Haviland, S. E., 10
Higgins, E. T., 8, 10, 11, 23, 71, 80
Hild, T., 52
Hilton, D. J., 20, 21, 22, 24, 25, 27, 85, 86
Hippler, H. J., 3, 35, 41, 43, 44, 45, 49, 51, 52, 56, 57, 58, 59, 60, 73

I

Inhelder, B., 64

J

James, W., 90
Jones, E. E., 3, 28

K

Kahneman, D., 3, 18, 19, 21, 23, 31, 85, 86
Kalton, G., 35
Kellenbenz, M., 4, 53
Kerker, R. M., 33, 37
Kihlstrom, J. F., 89, 90
Knäuper, B., 3, 41, 43, 44, 47
Kohlberg, L., 67
Krauss, R. M., 8
Krosnick, J. A., 26, 27, 28, 41, 87
Kruglanski, A. W., 88
Kübler, A., 71

L

Lakoff, R., 13
Lavallo, D., 31

Lehman, D. R., 26, 27
Lemley, R. H., 22
Letourneau, K. J., 68
Levinson, S. C., 8, 9, 11, 12, 13, 14, 83
Li, F., 26, 27, 28
Lichtenstein, S., 24
Light, P., 66
Loftus, E. F., 3, 33, 36
Lombardi, W. J., 71
Loosveldt, G., 52
Luttberg, N. R., 34

M

Mai, H. P., 4, 72, 76, 77, 79, 80, 81
Martin, E., 69
Martin, L. L., 34, 72, 75, 80, 81
Mason, R., 78, 81
McCann, C. D., 4, 8, 10, 11
McGarrigle, J., 65, 67
Menon, G., 52, 57
Meyer, C., 28
Miller, A. G., 28
Molenaar, N. J., 58
Molloy, C. G., 66
Monaco, G. E., 39
Müller, G., 50

N

Naderer, G., 20, 21, 22, 24, 25, 27, 86
Neilson, I., 66
Nisbett, R. E., 18, 28
Noelle-Neumann, E., 3, 41, 43, 44, 58

O

O'Muircheartaigh, C. A., 50, 52
Oldendick, R. W., 34, 59
Orne, M. T., 88, 89

P

Pendergrass, J., 48
Pepitone, A., 22
Piaget, J., 3, 64
Pratt, A. R., 66
Presser, S., 3, 34, 41, 57, 58, 59, 70
Prince, E. F., 10

Subject Index